TRANSFORMING TEACHING

Creating Lesson Plans for Child-Centered Learning in Preschool

Marie L. Masterson

National Association for the Education of Young Children
Washington, DC

National Association for the Education of Young Children

1401 H Street NW, Suite 600
Washington, DC 20005
202-232-8777 • 800-424-2460
NAEYC.org

NAEYC Books
**Senior Director, Publishing
and Professional Learning**
Susan Friedman

Director, Books
Dana Battaglia

Senior Editor
Holly Bohart

Editor
Rossella Procopio

Senior Creative Design Manager
Henrique J. Siblesz

Senior Creative Design Specialist
Gillian Frank

Senior Creative Design Specialist
Charity Coleman

**Publishing Business
Operations Manager**
Francine Markowitz

Through its publications program, the National Association for the Education of Young Children (NAEYC) provides a forum for discussion of major issues and ideas in the early childhood field, with the hope of provoking thought and promoting professional growth. The views expressed or implied in this book are not necessarily those of the Association.

Permissions

NAEYC accepts requests for limited use of our copyrighted material. For permission to reprint, adapt, translate, or otherwise reuse and repurpose content from this publication, review our guidelines at NAEYC.org/resources/permissions.

Photo and illustration credits

Copyright © Getty except as noted in the text.

**Transforming Teaching: Creating Lesson Plans
for Child-Centered Learning in Preschool**

Library of Congress Control Number: 2020945447

ISBN: 978-1-938113-83-3

Item: 1152

To Kathy Charner, who inspired the book in the first place; to the preschool educators who make a difference daily in the lives of children and families; and to my father, Gordon Mumma, with love and appreciation.

Contents

Introduction

When you think about writing lesson plans, what comes to mind? Maybe you use a daily schedule, track activities on a weekly calendar, and keep lists with materials and props for play areas. Maybe you work from a set of preschool standards and a sequence required by a curriculum, program, or school district. Maybe you also have tried-and-true activities that highlight special events or times of the year, such as a back-to-school focus or changing seasons. But what additional steps or ideas could improve your planning?

This book is designed to show what is possible when teachers use lesson planning as a prime mover for effective teaching. In engineering, a prime mover is a machine that receives energy input and transforms its source of power into useful work or motion (*Encyclopedia Britannica*, n.d.). In the same way, a lesson plan can become your creative and intentional machine to revitalize, energize, and organize the elements of effective, high-quality teaching.

No matter what lesson templates and processes you are currently using, this book offers new ways to improve planning and organization. Each chapter introduces real-life examples and shows what is possible when teachers work together to enrich and personalize teaching. Child-centered lesson planning can have a daily positive impact on your time and energy and on the quality of children's learning and engagement.

How Does Lesson Planning Fit into Everything?

Many teachers express the challenge of completing required planning, observation, and teaching. How do you tell what children are learning as they push buggies, slide shopping bags over their arms, and bump happily into each other? As children pretend to be rescue workers during dramatic play, will lesson planning enhance their learning? What can you do to strengthen language and social skills? The approach you choose will reflect the teaching philosophy of the program, the context of the families and community, and the learning needs of individual children.

Teaching priorities also reflect the increasing complexities of the field. Your focus must include specific learning goals, yet be flexible to meet the needs of children. You'll need to stay in step with what they are learning and doing today, yet keep in mind the skills they need tomorrow.

Weekly themes are a wonderful place to start your planning process. For example, a nature or gardening theme could proceed with Monday: Things that grow; Tuesday: Feeding birds; Wednesday: Planting seeds; etc. You may include songs, books, games, and other materials that relate to these concepts. For your science and nature area, you could provide dirt, gardening gloves, seed packets, trowels, watering cans, and small pots. For the dramatic play area, you might prepare a plant sale activity with a cash register, signs, price tags, and a receipt book. In this way, you begin to enhance children's learning during play.

Broader curricula can include project-based learning, units of study, and themes that can be divided into more specific topics. At the same time, additional conversations and activities may emerge from children's curiosity, interests, and ideas. All areas of development and learning must be strengthened in ways that are responsive to children's unique developmental, cultural, and linguistic characteristics.

Lesson planning can also help you become more effective in adapting to the needs of children. Perhaps a morning of play goes well, but you aren't sure why it worked. Maybe you see children struggle when playing in close proximity, but you don't know exactly what to change to make the materials and spaces work better. Maybe you want to introduce more creative book reading but aren't sure how to extend the concepts into play. A detailed lesson plan can help you make sense of each element of your setting—the interactions, materials, and activities—and make adjustments that actually make engagement easier and more successful for children.

How This Book Helps

This book offers a range of strategies that match what children are learning and doing. You may choose teacher-directed mini-lessons or facilitated group activities. You may jumpstart a short-term inquiry project to explore recycling or butterflies. The strategies will help you stock your toolbox with tips that enhance your teaching approach. No matter what strategies you adopt, be sure to support independent and collaborative play to extend and strengthen children's skills.

In each chapter, you will find step-by-step hints and action steps to make the most of your unique setting. You'll read about teachers who recognize each child's unique knowledge, skills, and cultural and linguistic experiences as assets for learning (NAEYC, 2020). You'll explore classrooms that reflect and strengthen children's "social identities, interests, strengths, and preferences; their personalities, motivations, and approaches to learning; and their knowledge, skills, and abilities related to their cultural experiences, including family languages, dialects, and vernaculars" (NAEYC, 2020, p.7). In addition, you will explore new ways to

> Build on early learning guidelines and standards to maximize planning and communication

> Identify learning goals for materials, activities, routines, and interactions

> Design dramatic play themes that relate to daily life, families, cultures, and communities

> Infuse rich vocabulary experiences to scaffold language development

> Support executive function skills and strengthen self-regulation

> Activate emotion coaching goals and effective behavior guidance

> Evaluate and adapt spaces and materials to address physical needs

> Meet the linguistic and social needs of dual language learners

> Prepare meaningful and stimulating cognitive experiences

> Connect content skills, language, and literacy to dramatic play

> Integrate family engagement as a strength and asset for development and learning

> Communicate effectively with colleagues to ensure high-quality learning experiences

The NAEYC Early Learning Program Accreditation Standards and Assessment Items (2018) provide an important foundation for high-quality experiences for young children. The content and lesson planning information presented in this book align with the NAEYC criteria as follows:

> It acknowledges the essential need for positive relationships between all children and adults to encourage each child's sense of worth and belonging as part of a community and to foster each child's ability to contribute as a responsible community member (Standard 1: Relationships).

> It supports the use of curriculum that is consistent with its goals for children and that promotes learning and development in each of the following areas: social, emotional, physical, language, and cognitive (Standard 2: Curriculum).

> It promotes the use of a variety of developmentally, culturally, and linguistically appropriate and effective teaching approaches that enhance each child's learning and development in the context of the program's curriculum goals (Standard 3: Teaching).

> It presents the use of a variety of formal and informal assessment approaches to provide information on children's learning and development. These assessments occur in the context of reciprocal communication between teachers and families and with sensitivity to the cultural context in which children are developing. It uses assessment results to inform decisions about children, to improve teaching practices, and to drive program improvement (Standard 4: Assessment of Child Progress).

> It ensures teachers establish and maintain collaborative relationships with each child's family to foster children's development in all settings. These relationships are sensitive to family composition, language, and culture (Standard 7: Families).

Chapter Features

Each chapter opens with a teaching scenario that sets the stage for the many features that follow in every chapter and invite you to dig deeper and apply what you read to your own setting. Additional teaching scenarios or classroom examples appearing throughout the chapters show teaching in action and represent a variety of preschool settings and situations. They demonstrate the principles and strategies in practical and useful ways.

Chapter features include:

> **Tips for teaching.**
This feature details practical skills to maximize your effectiveness in meeting children's learning and social needs. You will find ideas for preparation, observation, materials, vocabulary, supporting learning, encouraging children's choices, and making the most of teachable moments.

> **Research connections.**
Research on children's development drives the activities and interactions that will strengthen emerging skills. These easy-to-relate links will ensure you know the latest information.

> **Individualized teaching.**
This section will connect the development of children to their relationships with families, communities, and culture. Here you will also find considerations for children who are learning multiple languages.

> **Helpful hints.**
Quick suggestions show how to make lesson planning work for you.

> **Balance points.**
Sensitivity and responsiveness are essential during interactions with preschool children. Topics include using reflective practice, positive communication, behavior guidance during play, social-emotional learning, seeing from children's perspectives, and supporting self-regulation and positive behavior.

> **Ready resources.**
Sources for digging deeper are provided for early screening and intervention, adaptation for special needs, technical assistance networks, state early guidelines, creative activities, teaching resources, and national organizations.

> **Field notes.**
Teachers in the field share practical insights and strategies to make classroom organization and planning easier.

> **Links to NAEYC Early Learning Program Accreditation Standards and Assessment Items.**
This feature anchors curriculum planning, effective teaching, assessment, and family engagement to professional guidelines and high-quality practices.

> **Sample lesson plans.**
These materials include complete lesson plans with detailed vocabulary and concept strategies, book lists, individualization for children with special needs, support for multilingual learners, and thematic extensions for play areas.

> **Chapter reflection questions.**
Reflective practice questions at the end of each chapter will inspire your growth and can be used for personal study or group discussion.

If you are an experienced teacher, this book can help you to assess where you are and then experiment with new ideas. You may have a valued program philosophy that guides your priorities and teaching style. Use the resources in this book as a comprehensive approach or adopt parts that update and enrich your current strategies. Start with tools you already have and build on previous activities that worked well. Try a different strategy or add a new action step, but don't try to do everything at once. Implement ideas that inspire your work, feel "doable," and make sense for your unique activities, approach, and setting. Over time, small steps will inspire new creativity, energy, and effectiveness.

If you are just starting your career in teaching, this book will provide you with practical and inspiring foundations for a fulfilling life in the classroom and community. Each chapter will help you imagine, plan for, and implement effective teaching practices.

CHAPTER 1

Setting a Foundation for Teaching

Celebrating How Children Learn

Jorge wears a chef's hat at the sand table. He scoops and sprays sand with water. He packs it firmly into a plastic lid with his hand. "I'm making *pupusas con curtido (corn cakes)* for mama." Ms. Aria smiles. "What ingredients do you have?" Jorge answers, "Corn and water." Ms. Aria offers, "Here is a spatula. The flat blade will spread the dough. Then you can stuff the cabbage. Who is coming for dinner?" Jorge answers, "My sister." Ms. Aria says, "You can show Arabella how to cook dinner."

Ms. Aria plans play materials to match what children know. Jorge lives in the city with a large extended family from El Salvador. Often, Jorge's sisters pick him up from school. Ms. Aria knows the names of all the family members. Her cooking center includes tools like wooden *molinillos* to whisk coffee, a spatula for spreading *masa*, and a mortar and pestle for spices. The children use a lightweight griddle with many small bowls. These items are familiar to the children and inspire realistic play.

This week, the theme is helping others. Ms. Aria has specific goals in mind. She watches carefully to see how children use materials. She has written prompts and vocabulary words on a small card. She takes a clipboard with her to write notes about what the children say. A small digital camera fits into a pocket on the back of the clipboard. The children know she will use it to take pictures of them. Teaching requires a balance of active participation and holding back to see what children will do and say.

Ms. Aria's most effective teaching tool is observing children. Through observation, she learns as much from the children as they do from her. For example, during dramatic play, Emil tries to stack plastic cups by size. He struggles with the cups several times and sighs with frustration. Even though she is tempted to show Emil how the cups fit, Ms. Aria gently prompts, "What would happen if you try the blue cup first?" Emil grins as he inserts the red cup into the blue one. Ms. Aria responds to Emil's progress. She adds a collection of shells to the science area for Emil and the other children to sort by size and color. By observing emerging skills in one area, she can adjust the level of challenge and complexity in other areas of play to strengthen children's learning.

While Ms. Aria is an active participant, she waits to introduce a word or new way of using a prop until she finds a natural pause in the children's conversation.

She doesn't take over what the children are doing but follows their ideas. At times, she helps the children move a table or adjust the space to better support their work. As a play facilitator, she enjoys helping the children engage deeply in imaginative thinking. She helps children find costumes and props to act out characters and stories. She shows them how a box can be a train or a canoe and a scarf can be a cape or turban. She models different ways a pinecone makes interesting patterns when rolled in the sand. She provides markers for children to illustrate a shopping list of ingredients to make a fancy dish. The children are eager to be creative and apply what they know.

Ms. Aria draws the children together in a play circle after free choice time. She asks them to describe the best part of their play. There is a lot of laughter when Jorge says he burned the cabbage and set fire to the *pupusas*. He says Vania and Mario came to put out the fire. Louis and Max share how they argued during block play about the location for a helicopter port on the hospital roof, so they decided to turn the entire construction into an airport. The other children nod with understanding. The themes of helping and community service come to life when children share their stories. This play circle is a celebration of learning and fun.

TIPS FOR TEACHING
Learning by Observing

Teaching begins by learning from children. Children communicate their interests through play choices and by the props and books they enjoy. They show what they need by their enthusiasm for or hesitation to try new experiences. Children communicate both through what they are doing and through what they are not doing. For example, a child who plays with a shoelace during group reading may be more fully focused than a child who looks at you but needs encouragement to share her ideas. A child wiggling his leg during a fine motor activity may distract other children but is simply trying to contain his energy. You can provide additional space or encourage children to stand at the table rather than sit. You may see a child turn his body away to shield a toy. That's the time to help him use words to express his needs and to provide additional materials. When children stand alone or are not fully engaged, they show the need for support. Their words, facial expressions, and body language show whether they can manage a situation well or whether they are struggling to cope.

Understanding physical cues takes practice. You need to know each child well and respond in positive, sensitive ways to build their competence. What are you looking for when you observe children? The following questions will help you tune in more fully and set a clear purpose for observation:

> **Are there specific skill objectives you want to be sure children attempt or master?** What manipulatives and games will foster understanding of a math concept? What areas of phonemic awareness need to be strengthened through repeatable books, songs, or word games? Will inviting children to gather natural objects increase their interest in science journal drawings?

> **Do you want to see how children solve problems, monitor tasks, complete projects, approach situations, or interact with others?** What ingredients of the setting, social interactions, space, or time restraints are influencing children's behavior? What strategies are children using to solve learning or social challenges?

> **What similarities or patterns do you notice?** Do children ask for help before getting frustrated? Do they work independently or cooperate for longer periods of time? Do they show increasing ability to communicate their thinking and ideas? Are there changes in physical skills or behavior regulation? Are some areas of development moving ahead of others?

> **What capabilities and interests do you see?** Do verbal skills keep pace with children's needs so they can communicate about what they want? Are fine motor skills strong enough for a specific activity? Do you notice new interests, questions, and ideas?

> **What kind of support is needed?** What questions will encourage deeper thinking? Are there additional concepts or skills you can model? What vocabulary will enhance children's ideas? Do you need to teach or review social skills or problem-solving approaches?

> **What factors contribute to the success of an activity?** Do children have ample space to move freely? Are enough materials present to support the type of play and number of children? Is there a balance of active and quiet play choices? Is there a range of complexity and skill levels to meet the needs of all children?

> **What is the best way to document what you see?** What do children do or say that shows how they think? What do children say about their activity? What specific notes will capture the emerging skills you see? What "next skills" do you want to introduce to boost knowledge, understanding, or competence?

To support the needs of children, listen, observe, and adapt your responses to make the most of teaching moments. For example, during recess, children notice trees have shaggy and smooth bark. Build on their curiosity and introduce *Trees, Leaves, and Bark*, by Diane L. Burns, or another picture book to explore in the science area. Evaluate the way they respond and engage. You can use this information to strengthen your lesson planning choices.

Field Note: Being My Best Self

Teaching is all about the children. But it's also about me. To stay tuned in, I need to be rested and alert. To have meaningful conversations, I need positive energy and focus. I want to be creative and have impact. Just thirty minutes of extra sleep each night makes a difference. Packing healthy snacks on the weekend helps, too. A book club with colleagues keeps me motivated. When I write lesson plans, I'm inspired to be my best self so children can be their best selves. I want them to grow up with the traits they see in me, like creativity, patience, and curiosity.

Helping Children Thrive with Developmentally Appropriate Practice

> Ms. Mona tells a story to the children about José and his brother. The boys and their uncle take the bus to *el mercado de pescado,* the local fish market. It is their grandmother's birthday and many relatives are coming. The boys tell the storekeeper their mother needs shrimp, saffron, and parsley. They carry the package, pay the bus fare, and travel home. As the children hurry through the front door, they smell the aroma of savory rice. They hug their mother and grandmother.

> When the story is finished, Ms. Mona asks the children, "How do you help your family?" Hayden answers, "Mmm. My house smells good. I help mamá eat food." The children laugh with appreciation. Miguel adds, "I help mamá with our baby." Ms. Mona says, "Our families depend on us to help."

Ms. Mona wants the children to understand that families help each other. She begins by talking about something these children know well—taking the bus to the market. Ms. Mona knows the children enjoy weekend meals with relatives. Importantly, she wants the children to recognize themselves in the stories and ideas.

NAEYC's position statement "Developmentally Appropriate Practice" (2020) was revised to reflect a strengths-based approach to teaching. Teachers must understand that there are many contributions to children's learning and development, and children are most motivated to learn when they feel a sense of belonging, identity, and value in their classroom community.

A core component of developmentally appropriate practice (DAP) is honoring the personal experiences children have with their families. Experiences must be meaningful, relevant, and respectful to each child and family. This context allows children to identify with and take pride in learning. NAEYC explains that teachers must "fully consider the specific abilities, interests, experiences, and motivations of a particular child or their family's culture, preferences, values, and child-rearing practices" (NAEYC 2020, 34).

Developmentally appropriate practice requires deep insight into the ways children develop and learn. It involves knowing how emerging skills build on previous skills. Teachers need to recognize skills as they are emerging and what kind of activities and supports can promote learning. Knowing what is individually and culturally appropriate will help ensure each child achieves challenging and achievable learning goals.

The DAP revision moves away from the idea of one "best practice." It notes that, "Educators who rely on the notion of a single 'best' practice often make assumptions based on their own experiences, which may not have involved extensive experiences with a variety of populations. These assumptions can be biased if they do not fully consider the specific abilities, interests, experiences, and motivations of a particular child or their family's culture, preferences, values, and child-rearing practices when determining the most appropriate practice for that child" (34). It also requires decisions that are "informed by evidence, research, and professional judgement" and alignment to the NAEYC Professional Standards and Competencies for Early Childhood Educators. Per the position statement, "building on each child's strengths—and taking care to not harm any aspect of each child's physical, cognitive, social, or emotional well-being—educators design and implement learning settings to help each child achieve their full potential across all domains of development and across all content areas" (5). Developmentally appropriate practice relies on

sensitivity and inclusiveness toward families as well as responsiveness to a wide range of diversities, including children's skills, abilities, experiences, languages, and dialects. It requires an "extensive repertoire of skills and a dynamic knowledge base to make decisions, sometimes balancing what at first appear to be contradictory demands, in order to address this wide range of diversity" (34). Using developmentally appropriate practice, you will continue to grow and learn about the specific needs of children and families in your own unique setting and community.

Developmentally appropriate practice ensures

> Respect for children's lives and daily experiences

> Knowledge of children to build on their strengths and assets

> Teaching experiences that fit with the lives of children and the ways they learn best

> Teaching strategies that are individualized to the needs of each child

> A meaningful context for learning that fits with each child's sense of self

> A sense of belonging and pride children hold for themselves, their families, and their community

Developmentally appropriate practice empowers teachers to be more effective. When you focus the lens of DAP, you can see the moment-by-moment perspective of each child. When you prepare an activity, consider what it looks like to him or her. Is it too complicated or too easy? Do your instructions make sense? Are the materials arranged in a user-friendly way? Do your words and demonstration of materials feel inviting and interesting to this child? What feelings, daily experiences, and family events connect to the new information you present? These questions are essential as you invite children to feel safe and participate fully.

Using Reflective Practice

Mildred and James, teachers in adjoining pre-K classrooms, meet after the children leave on Thursdays. They alternate rooms so they can help each other in practical ways. Mildred says, "With the new accessories, more than three children want to be in the block area. Can you help me enlarge the space?"

As they move blocks and push back the shelf unit, James shares a concern. "When I host family conferences at school," he says, "and family members are with me in the classroom, I feel comfortable and in control. When I visit families in their homes, I feel less secure. I was very excited to share a child's achievement during a recent home visit. Because my wonderful student was with us in the living room, I wanted to compliment him directly. I said, 'Way to go boy!' Then I could sense his family's discomfort. I immediately apologized, and the family was very kind. Until it happened, I didn't consider how using the word 'boy' might convey a derogatory meaning. I talked with a mentor afterward and read several articles to help me learn more about bias-free communication. I want to avoid using stereotypical language in the future and think carefully before I speak. What would you think about requesting this topic for an upcoming faculty meeting?"

Mildred responds, "I am sorry. I know how much power we have in the way we use words. Let's tell Mr. Cretser that we would like to make this topic a priority on the agenda. Why don't we ask for a full conversation about anti-bias teaching? I have wanted to introduce anti-bias curriculum and conversations more systematically in my classroom."

Because Mildred and James meet often, they touch on subjects that are personal and profound and that impact their teaching choices. They feel safe introducing topics that are challenging. They have come to value each other's feedback and support.

Ongoing reflection is the foundation of developmentally appropriate practice. Personal beliefs and assumptions influence teaching decisions, especially as you interact with children who have disabilities and teach children from different linguistic and cultural backgrounds than your own (Kucharczyk, Sreckovic, & Schultz 2019; Madrid Akpovo 2019; Whittingham, Hoffman, & Rumenapp 2018). Reflective practice is essential to ensure nonbiased expectations and positive support for children from differing racial backgrounds (Jacobsen, Pace, & Ramirez 2019; Peguero et al. 2015). Reflection includes identifying assumptions, evaluating teaching decisions and their impact, and understanding factors that influence children's learning, with flexibility and willingness to create positive change. Talking with colleagues can help you explore insights about your thinking and practice.

Intentional reflection with colleagues can make hidden viewpoints visible and aid in shifting to strengths-based assumptions and beliefs. This insight begins with reflection, open-mindedness, curiosity, and cultural empathy (Cushner & Chang 2015). Reflection helps you shift beyond a "right or best" way to teach to explore the strengths and needs of each child and the role of culture in children's lives.

Reflective practice ensures you take time to know children and their families well. It involves asking families about their hopes and goals for children. And it requires that expectations between home and your classroom setting make sense. For example, you'll ask families to guide you about the kinds of culturally relevant experiences to integrate during play. Look for books that match what children know and love. This kind of practice will inspire you to consider new ways of teaching and planning.

Reflective practice requires intentional focus and time. The goal may be to brainstorm solutions to current challenges or to learn new skills. While reflective practice is part of individual growth, insights from others can bring to light unexamined issues or make dilemmas visible. A great way to jumpstart your growth is to meet regularly with colleagues and invite feedback from families. Reflective practice can include recording insights in a journal or reviewing video of your teaching. It might include small group meetings that focus on requested topics, inviting professional experts to answer questions, or a small group book club. A community of practice can offer systematic exploration of new topics with the goal of shared growth. Importantly, reflective practice requires a mindset of flexibility and commitment to positive change. This open collaboration pays off in incredible gains as you understand children's needs more deeply and become a more compassionate and responsive teacher.

Connecting Teaching to Children's Lives

Ms. Lauren's class visits the children's museum to see a Mo Willems story exhibit. After the children interact with the book characters and watch their animated adventures, Ms. Lauren invites them to illustrate and record their own stories.

Ethan holds up his drawing of an enormous purple-and-red bird. "My pigeon drove the bus and took the children to school." Jada shows her picture, "My pigeon invited her friends to the library. They read every book on the shelf and made a gigantic pile on the floor. Their mothers had to pick up the mess."

Ms. Lauren knows the museum visit motivates the children's storytelling. The trip gives the children a firsthand look at bringing book characters to life. Ms. Lauren wants them to take pride in telling stories. She uses digital video to document the children's drawings and storytelling. She includes the videos in the children's portfolios and shares them with families. The children's own stories reflect their real-life experience at the museum.

Responsive teaching connects learning to children's lives. Children recognize their experiences in the curriculum, materials, and activities. During field trips, stories, play, and conversations, children learn about their peers, the world, and themselves (Bennett et al. 2018). Culture includes much more than food, festivals, and clothing. Curriculum content and images reflect diverse races, ethnicities, languages, social contexts, gender, age, and abilities. Books and displays show familiar illustrations and stories and communicate positive messages about children's lives. Teachers encourage children to take pride in their families and neighborhoods. These strengths and assets provide a context for children's sense of identity and belonging. Culture impacts children's developing sense of themselves and their world (Guo 2015).

Culture influences the way teachers ask questions, their beliefs about responsibility and compliance, and how quickly they step in to assist children (Gibbs 2005). Culture influences teachers' expectations about how children should collaborate, communicate, and problem solve (Bornstein 2013). Culture impacts beliefs about child rearing and whether teachers expect immediate compliance from children or take a more democratic approach to decision making (Rasaol, Eklund, & Hansen 2011). These beliefs are often unexamined but can influence teaching choices.

For families, culture influences perceptions of power, prestige given to teachers, and mindsets about speaking up or keeping things to oneself (Calzada et al. 2015). Cultural norms impact the way children "tune in" to adults or stay absorbed in their own thinking and actions. Culture impacts the sense of familiarity or formality with which people interact with others.

When you work with children from a different culture, ethnicity, or who speak a different language than your own, it is important to learn all you can about differing expectations and values. This can happen through your own research, through conversations with a "cultural broker" who knows the family or community well, and through conversation with families and children (Massing, Kirova, & Henning 2013). Open communication with colleagues and families promotes essential growth and understanding.

INDIVIDUALIZED TEACHING

Using a Strengths-Based Approach

Mr. Jasper reads *Frederick* and *A Color of His Own*, both by Leo Lionni, to the children. He asks them to talk about the meaning of *meadow, dreaming, hideout,* and *artist.* Mr. Jasper says that Leo Lionni is an artist who uses colors to tell stories. The children say they are artists when they paint pictures. After story time, the children are excited about using the easel. Mr. Jasper invites Esmeralda to talk about her painting. "Tell me about the beautiful colors." Esmeralda explains, "It's a sunset. The black is a cloud and orange is the sun." Mr. Jasper says, "You are like Frederick, storing up colors for the winter." Esmeralda says, "My mom is an artist. She paints pictures of me." Mr. Jasper nods. "You are an artist like your mom. She will love to see your beautiful colors."

Mr. Jasper hears the pride in Esmeralda's voice. Using the word *artist* gives importance to her painting. He wants Esmeralda to recognize the value of her creativity.

A *strengths-based approach* embraces the life values, resources, knowledge and social networks of families and children. A focus on strengths shifts away from a deficit mindset. Instead of seeing families as "disadvantaged," you can view families as fully functioning within a unique cultural setting (Velez-Ibanez 1988; Wolf 1966).

This approach is especially important when there are multiple perspectives and values present in a program. A strengths-based viewpoint does not assume limitations due to poverty or cultural or socioeconomic status. A strengths-based approach shifts from the idea that there is a "right" way of doing things to seeing families as fully competent in raising their children.

Strengths-based thinking leads to strengths-based language and communication. Words are powerful and convey indelible messages about children and families. Positive communication focuses on what children are learning and highlights positive steps toward growth. Positive communication promotes genuine regard and respect for the experiences and perspectives of others. Strengths-based communication will be discussed in detail in Chapter 6.

READY RESOURCES

Exploring Your Community Context

Take time to learn about your community, families, and children. The more you know, the more effective you will become in communication and teaching. Learning about others doesn't happen all at once; it is part of a journey of understanding that comes from many conversations, exploration of the community, and reflection about the contributions to people's lives. As you think about your community, ask the following questions:

> What is the history of the area?

> What positive resources are available to families and children?

> What are the unique strengths and cultural assets of the children's families?

> What can you learn about the numbers of multilingual families and children?

> What cultural and linguistic backgrounds are represented?

> In what new ways can you build on family values, strengths, and experiences?

The following are resources to explore:

> Early Childhood Training and Technical Assistance System Data Explorer and State Profiles: https://childcareta.acf.hhs.gov/data

> National Center for Children in Poverty State Profiles: www.nccp.org/profiles

> National Institute for Early Education Research State of Preschool Yearbooks: http://nieer.org/state-preschool-yearbooks

> National Center for Education Statistics Fast Facts—English Language Learners: https://nces.ed.gov/fastfacts/display.asp?id=96

> Child Care Aware of America State by State Resources: www.childcareaware.org/resources/map

> NAEYC "Developmentally Appropriate Practice" Position Statement: NAEYC.org/resources/position-statements/dap

Understanding the Role of Play in Development

At the fine motor table, Ravae and Izzy insert pegs into pegboards. Ravae says, "I'm making a cake." Izzy helps pull out a peg that is stuck. She says, "Put the red ones here 'cause you are five. You need five candles. The white ones go there." Izzy arranges a square of white pegs. Ravae fills the middle with blue pegs.

Ravae and Izzy practice much more than fine motor skills. They use persistence, problem solving, and intentional planning, essential competencies for school success. What looks like a simple activity promotes listening and cooperation as the girls work together and shift their plans to fit with each other's ideas. They tell stories and take turns. They sort, pattern, arrange, and design. Play provides fun with benefits.

During play, children experiment with objects to see how they work. Blocks inspire engineering experiments. Natural collections draw children into comparative investigations. Make-believe play strengthens communication. Ramp play teaches the rules of gravity as balls roll down slopes. Children learn about density and weight as they lift, sort, and stack objects. Play offers complex and interesting ways for children to discover and learn.

Play has a positive impact on many areas of children's development and learning:

> Play promotes all areas of development including social-emotional skills, self-regulation, executive function, and prosocial behaviors (Yogman et al. 2018).

> Play fosters curiosity, self-discovery, and creativity (Berke 2016).

> Outdoor play exposes children to rich opportunities for real-world learning, social interaction and collaboration, appropriate risk taking, and STEM (science, technology, engineering, and mathematics) skills (Kinsner 2019).

> Extended play experiences are essential for mediating stress and contribute to the development of self-regulation (Foley 2017).

> Dramatic play helps children explore and understand problems, situations, and themes as they reenact daily life scenarios. Play helps children develop symbolic thinking and explore concepts and new ideas (Brown 2017).

> Dramatic play connects learning to children's prior knowledge and cultural contexts (Karabon 2017).

> Play promotes language, cognitive, and social skills that are critical to academic success (Spiewak Toub et al. 2018).

> Active (or big body) play, construction play, and functional play strengthen a range of physical, gross and fine motor, and practical life skills (Lillard et al. 2013).

During play, children interact with adults to make meaning (Cutter-Mackenzie & Edwards 2013). They make sense by doing, trying, revising, and discussing their efforts (Hamlin & Wisneski 2012). Children try out ideas and test their hypotheses using processes of scientific inquiry. Play engages children in meaningful learning and is a critical pedagogical tool for teaching (Barblett, Knaus, & Barratt-Pugh 2016).

Supporting Families in Encouraging Playful Learning

There are many ways for teachers to help families enrich home-based play that will be appreciated during summer months, extended times of quarantine, and weekends. Activities may correlate with lesson plans or simply help families understand the thinking skills, content knowledge, and developmental strengths that children gain through play. Families will appreciate receiving tips through text, email, or your program's digital application. Below are some simple suggestions for how families can engage children more meaningfully in play-based learning:

> Ask questions about children's play plans and play needs (e.g., to be a firefighter, create a store, make a restaurant). "What will you do first? How will you make that happen? What materials and props do you need to carry out your play ideas?"

> Respond to children's questions with informational materials (e.g., provide a book that shows breeds of dogs and ways of caring for animals to a child who helps feed the family pet at home).

> Add interesting measuring tools, tubes, and funnels during water play and bath time and ask questions like, "What will happen if . . . ?" and "Which container holds more (less)?"

> Include children in cooking and baking activities to support measuring, pouring, comparing, planning, and communication skills.

> Inspire nature play by talking about animals in the yard, feeding birds, and providing informational books. Offer containers for children to collect natural materials (like bark, leaves, pinecones, and seed pods) to then sort, study, and draw.

> Promote art play by providing full-color magazine pictures (e.g., healthy foods, colors, sports items) for children to use for collages, preparing homemade playdough with salt and flour, offering table space for watercolor painting, and providing empty boxes for painting or decorating.

> Enjoy simple card and board games, which teach important mathematics, reasoning, and social skills.

> Use educational technology well. Enjoy online book reading, painting demonstrations, and science shows designed just for children. Respond by helping children gather materials to carry out the play activities they have observed.

Teaching with Children in Mind

Nathalie and Atlas disagree about which box should go first as they line them up to make a train. Mathias interrupts, "Use the big box for the engine. The long one can be the caboose." Ms. Geweria responds, "That's a good solution. What do you think, Atlas?" Atlas nods.

Ms. Geweria asks, "Will you please hold the box steady while I cut the door?" Atlas and Mathias hold the box as she uses the scissors. Ms. Geweria asks, "Will this be a freight train or a passenger train? Do you need markers to make windows on the passenger train?" She offers the container and the children select colors. "I'm making the ladder," announces Atlas. "Okay," says Nathalie. "I'm making the control panel." "I'm making mine orange," says Mathias. "It takes teamwork to reach your goals," adds Ms. Geweria. "You are making a long passenger train."

Ms. Geweria wants the children to understand and use vocabulary like *passenger* and *freight* to expand their thinking about trains. She knows arranging and decorating the boxes challenge their fine motor skills. She encourages Mathias's ideas and stays near to support the children's progress.

Individualized teaching addresses the needs of specific children. *Individualized* means tailoring your choices, supports, and interactions to ensure the specific child can be successful and take pride in learning. It involves making practical adjustments to activities, time, materials, goals, and levels of support. You ensure children have access to materials and can participate fully. Individualization means knowing children well and supporting their success.

Individualized support is important for all preschool children. It involves keeping track of skills children can carry out independently and identifying skills that are still developing and need support.

Goals for individualization may focus on any area of development, including physical, cognitive, language, social, and motor skills. You will address specific areas of development when a child has an individualized education program (IEP). Consider the following scenario:

Mr. Joshua sits quietly next to Adam, stretching a length of bright red yarn between his hands. Adam snips the yarn with his scissors. Mr. Joshua slides over the yarn to create a new length so Adam can cut again. Adam loves this game and doesn't realize it is planned to provide practice with fine motor skills. They spend just a few minutes together before Adam moves on to a collage activity. This brief time of individualization was written into the lesson plan, but it seems to Adam like a natural, enjoyable part of play.

The following are examples of individualization that benefit children with and without an IEP:

> Modeling how to count vegetables for "purchase" during dramatic play and assisting a child with each step until she can do it independently

> Spending time with a child scaffolding and supporting specific emerging skills

> Creating a notebook about a child's favorite interest, such as breeds of dogs, to help her identify letters and letter sounds

> Adhering paper to a work table with masking tape so the paper won't slide when a child draws

> Adding grips or knobs to puzzles, toys, and other objects for ease of manipulation

> Offering a variety of shapes and sizes for art, writing, and science tools

> Including individual and large print books

> Providing additional space at a table or a mat to differentiate space

> Inviting multiple ways to answer questions, such as giving a thumbs up, writing on a lap board, or pairing with a partner to decide

> Offering additional or flexible time to continue or complete a project

> Giving choices about ways to demonstrate learning, such as making a poster board, performing a skit, telling a story, or explaining a skill

> Modifying learning goals to decrease or increase complexity or challenge

> Ensuring close supervision to monitor problem solving and cooperation during activities

Even after planning specific supports, continue to pay attention to the way children respond to experiences. Notice if there are barriers to engagement and adjustments that can facilitate play. Children should be able to reach and use materials independently. Moving a shelf back or shifting the location of a table can allow children to access materials easily. Make sure children have enough space to work and can find the materials they need. For example, costumes and props may be stuffed together in a basket. Instead, organize materials to support a specific theme or pretend play activity. Train hats, a basket of tickets, receipt books, money, and maps stored together help children reenact train travel. For airplane play, suitcases, passports, and "snacks" can be added, along with small bags and hats. It helps to evaluate spaces and materials during play to see what works well and facilitates prolonged focus and engagement.

HELPFUL HINT

Following the Children's Lead

While you have specific teaching goals in mind, lesson planning also allows you to be flexible and follow the children's lead. Be sure to include written notes, insights, and ongoing updates to your lesson plans. Consider the following questions:

> What else can enhance a lesson or activity that relates to a specific child's interest or ideas?

> Have parents mentioned family events that can be linked to new information you introduce?

> Have children asked questions that you can follow up on by providing informational books, videos, materials, or activities?

> What questions have children raised for which you need to explore more information or locate more resources?

As you monitor play activities, take notes about what you observe to inform your lesson plan: lists of props to add, questions children asked, and additional resources you want to explore. Since many activities take place over multiple days, adding on to your plan creates a template for you to use as a living document to improve and adapt your teaching.

RESEARCH CONNECTIONS

Strategies for Inclusion

Inclusive preschool programs teach children with disabilities in classrooms alongside their typically developing peers (ED & HHS 2015). Inclusive practices offer a range of benefits, including promoting nondiscriminatory practices and attitudes as well as fostering higher levels of achievement (McKee & Friedlander 2017). Children develop greater empathy and acceptance for each other (Lohmann 2017). Inclusive teaching is especially important during early childhood, as all young children present a range of developmental skills and needs. Individualized planning and practical support for each child is critical.

Universal design for learning is an educational framework that ensures that all children feel included, have full access to materials and spaces, and can engage in indoor and outdoor activities (CAST 2019). Universal design for learning examines the why, what, and how of learning to ensure barriers are removed and all children can experience success. Three principles of universal design for learning include

> **Representation**: Teachers share information in more than one way to promote understanding.

> **Expression**: Teachers show children more than one way to interact with materials and encourage many ways to demonstrate their learning.

> **Engagement**: Teachers use practical and meaningful ways to include and motivate students.

Universal design for learning is especially important for young children who display a wide range of needs, abilities, developmental patterns, and linguistic and cultural backgrounds (Dinnebeil, Boat, & Bae 2013). It includes modifications to physical spaces and adaptation of materials. Importantly, it requires practical daily responsiveness to children to see what can be added, adjusted, or modified to support their development and learning.

Differentiation is a teaching method that allows all children to reach learning goals by providing entry points, learning tasks, and outcomes tailored to individual learning needs (Watts-Taffe et al. 2012). Differentiation strategies include offering multiple ways of presenting content, creating flexible grouping, adjusting the pace, and offering choices (Gadzikowski 2016). For example, you may introduce a counting game during a focused one-on-one interaction. You may read to several children together to increase their interest in books. You may lead a small group graphing activity or facilitate a large group science activity. Differentiation ensures your instructional choices match the purpose of the activity and the needs of children.

Examples of differentiation include

> Introducing ideas or concepts in multiple ways, like demonstrating shape sorting during group instruction, adding sorting materials to fine motor play, and discussing shapes during snack

> Adding items to dramatic play that represent children's daily lives at home

> Labeling objects in the home languages of children as well as in English

> Choosing books that reflect the many diversities of families and their activities

> Offering play objects that provide a range of challenge, skill, and complexity, such as puzzles with fewer pieces and those with more complex patterns

> Providing informational books and activities that address children's specific interests and provide answers to their questions

> Engaging children during play activities to extend their thinking about concepts and vocabulary

> Using individual, small group, and large group activities to maximize children's engagement and interest.

Exploring Elements of Child-Centered Teaching

Jack and Miranda stack yogurt containers and tubes to make robots. They stick them together with bits of masking tape. Mr. George notices Miranda's tower keeps tipping. As he sees her struggle, he offers to hold the bottom cartons steady while she manages the tape. Miranda sticks on the pieces of tape, and the containers stay upright.

"Tell me about your robot," prompts Mr. George. "Mine is a police robot," states Miranda. "It can stop speeding cars." Mr. George asks, "How will your robot travel?" Miranda answers, "He has wheels that pop out of his feet." "I got a transformer robot," says Jack. "How will your robot travel?" Mr. George asks. Jack smiles, "My robot will turn into a racecar and drive fast."

Mr. George asks questions to explore the children's thinking about the way their creations move and travel. He has prepared materials and questions. He watches carefully to see how children experiment and learn. He intervenes gently to help problem solve.

When children are engrossed in play, you may step aside to observe and document what they are doing. Children need space and time to figure things out. At other times, you may plan a scripted activity such as a puppet show, a reading activity, or a science experiment. Your approach must be matched to the purpose or learning goals of the activity and to the needs of the children. Some situations require greater autonomy and others require greater levels of support.

In child-centered pedagogy, teachers and children together are fully engaged partners during the learning processes of exploration, problem solving, and creativity (Nilsson, Ferholt, & Lecusay 2018). Children interact with teachers during conversations and share their thinking while they explore and work (Siraj-Blatchford 2009). They participate in sustained, shared thinking with adults and peers as they focus together on a play activity or goal (Degotardi 2017). This relationship-based, socially active approach develops and extends children's understanding.

Child-centered teaching is proactive (Hedges & Cooper 2018). Prepared play areas serve a purpose for learning. For example, sand trays with a range of natural objects (e.g., shells, feathers, pebbles, and pinecones) and small tools invite children to compare textures and patterns, strengthen fine motor skills, and express creativity. You can demonstrate various ways to use the materials. Prepare a card with descriptive vocabulary to model, including *straight, smooth, swirl, same, different, pattern,* and *zigzag,* and position words like *above, below, middle,* and *between.* Add questions and prompts, such as "Which objects make a wavy (straight) pattern?" "Tell me about your favorite pattern," and "What shapes did you design?" Intentional, child-centered interactions promote thinking, problem solving, language skills, and peer conversations (Whorrall & Cabell 2016). Purposeful scaffolding becomes a powerful tool to strengthen learning (Edwards 2017).

Child-centered teaching creates a rich context for multilingual learners. Strategies include using children's home languages as a resource, engaging in play with children to model and support new vocabulary, demonstrating what words mean, clarifying what children say, and expanding on children's comments (Chapman de Sousa 2019).

There are many benefits of learning two or more languages, including stronger executive function skills, cognitive development, social-emotional competence, accelerated learning, and long-term school and career success (Julius 2018). Child-centered teaching is responsive and personal, and it values the contributions and perspectives of all children.

Child-centered teaching involves families and depends on authentic and meaningful family engagement. Families are valued as essential partners in goal setting and decision making about children's development and learning. Effective child-centered teaching requires understanding and valuing the race, language, and cultural backgrounds of children and their families (BUILD Initiative 2019). Family communication provides essential information, feedback, and support to plan curriculum, activities, and individualized scaffolding for children's success.

Child-centered teaching builds skills. It considers all contributions to learning and behavior, including spaces, materials, activities, and supports that ensure children's success. Children must have easy access to materials and opportunities to make choices and take initiative. Children need to know and do a lot! You, in turn, will need to know

› The practical skills children need to engage successfully in learning and play activities

› The physical and regulation skills children need for self-care and indoor and outdoor routines and transitions

› The developmental skills that emerge over time so you can keep track of new and beginning skills and design supporting activities

› The academic and content area skills children will learn during the year in order to plan activities and scaffold learning

In this way, child-centered teaching builds on children's development and engages them fully throughout daily activities. It takes into consideration all areas of development and offers a positive, encouraging setting for growth. Child-centered teaching ensures a safe and happy place for children to learn.

Sample Lesson Plans

Planning a Child-Centered Daily Schedule

A block schedule keeps you on track and ensures maximum time for learning with minimum time wasted during transitions. This approach provides broad time frames, during which children have a range of choices for uninterrupted play. Rather than schedule specific times for topic areas, you will be able to embed content learning in a variety of activities and events throughout the day. You can plan a range of experiences, including one-on-one, small group, and large group activities. For reading and teaching activities, you'll have a variety of choices about where and how you introduce skills and extend these concepts into play.

A block schedule provides consistent structure yet allows flexibility. You plan focused child-discovery activities, child-directed play, emergent learning projects, teacher-guided introductions, and teacher-directed lessons to support your goals. For example, during the morning greeting when families bring children to the classroom, child-discovery learning activities are prepared to support children's transition to the classroom setting. During extended free-choice periods, children participate in child-guided learning as they pursue play activities. A well-planned schedule assists you in planning the type of activity and level of support that matches the learning goals and objectives and takes into consideration the learning needs of the specific children you teach.

The written block schedules shown in Figure 1.1 represent flexible-use time. The blocks are suggestive, rather than prescriptive. Notice that bathroom and self-care routines are not indicated so that transition time is minimized. Children can attend to self-care as needed with sensitive and responsive teacher support. Time indications are mapped out for the purpose of lesson planning and to maximize opportunities for learning throughout the day.

Licensing regulations require preschoolers (children ages 3 to 5) to have one trained adult for six to 10 children, with no more than 20 preschoolers per classroom. At least two teachers must be present at all times (Administration for Children and Families, Office of Child Care, n.d.). The schedules are based on the presence of at least two teachers available to greet families, monitor activities, and facilitate children's play and learning. Responsibilities as indicated should be divided to ensure effective coverage of tasks and teaching needs.

Circle time is indicated for 30 minutes in the first example and for 20 minutes in the second example. This should be a flexible block of time that is adapted to the developmental needs and capabilities of the specific children you teach. During this time, *children are not expected to sit still for 20 or 30 minutes*. As long as children are actively engaged, teachers may facilitate music and movement play, book reading, interactive conversations, social-emotional learning, math and science demonstrations, classroom guests, and other response activities.

All activities should be modified and enriched to meet each child's needs. Alternative activities and meaningful supports like individual books, hands-on materials, and varied pacing should be available to ensure that all children have choices and can participate successfully.

Keeping these goals in mind, you'll need to know your children well, so that interactive toys and materials are appropriately challenging. You will plan for a variety of responsive experiences throughout each day. You will want to change the setting and supports of your classroom as children develop and mature over time.

A consistent schedule with well-planned activities stabilizes children's experience, minimizes stress, and ensures the best opportunities for learning. Whether programs teach children in person or provide alternative learning activities for remote learning, all children will benefit from predictable, yet flexible structure to gain competence and feel secure.

Sample Schedules

Sample 1: Half-Day Preschool Program	
7:30–8:30 am	Greeting and child-discovery activities Includes family greetings, hand washing, one-on-one reading, small group play, art activities, and play activities. In some programs, this time includes breakfast.
8:30–9 am	Morning circle Includes targeted skills, such as calendar, weather graphing, numbers and math activity, reading and writing workshop, science focus, social-emotional learning, or phonemic awareness, phonics, and letter play. May include rhythm, music, and movement with focus on multicultural awareness. Includes morning jobs as transition. Time and activities are modified to the engagement and developmental needs of children.
9–9:45 am	Gross motor play (outdoors, weather permitting) Includes freestanding equipment as well as portable equipment to build skills. Alternative indoor space is used when weather does not permit outdoor play.
9:45–10 am	Large and small group focus activities Includes whole-group reading, writing, or intensive content skill focus. Integrates themes from books and author studies, social-emotional learning, and content learning in interactive formats.
10–11:30 am	Free choice play All learning areas are open with access to prepared play areas, including reading, writing, dramatic play, art, music and movement, blocks, fine motor/manipulatives, math, science and nature (including sand and water), and additional sensory or open-ended projects. Snack is incorporated as free choice and monitored by a teacher.
11:30 am–Noon	Mini-skill building units with flexible grouping Includes storytelling, art and music exploration, science and STEM, math games, and book reading. Options include one-on-one conferencing, small group, and large group formats.
Noon–12:10 pm	Closing ritual with great moments and song
12:15 pm	Dismissal and family greeting

Sample 2: Full-Day Preschool Program	
8:10–8:30 am	Breakfast Breakfast takes place inside the classroom but may be located in a common program area. When located in the classroom, children select books or a quiet play activity when finished with breakfast as a transition to the morning circle.
8:30–8:50 am	Morning circle Includes targeted skills, such as calendar, weather graphing, numbers and math activity, reading and writing workshop, science focus, social-emotional learning, or phonemic awareness, phonics, and letter play. May include rhythm, music, and movement with focus on multicultural awareness. Includes morning jobs as transition. Time and activities are modified to the engagement and developmental needs of children.
8:50–9:50 am	Free choice play All learning areas are open with access to prepared play areas, including reading, writing, dramatic play, art, music and movement, blocks, fine motor/manipulatives, math, science and nature (including sand and water), and additional sensory or open-ended projects. Snack is incorporated as free choice and monitored by a teacher.
9:55–10:40 am	Gross motor play (outdoors, weather permitting) Includes freestanding equipment as well as portable equipment to build skills. Alternative indoor space is used when weather does not permit outdoor play.
10:40–11 am	Flexible learning time for self-care and learning Options include large group reading, phonemic awareness games, or math activities.
11–11:40 am	Lunch
11:40 am–1 pm	Soothing nap routine and sleeping
1–1:20 pm	Small group, individual, and quiet play Includes one-on-one book reading, reading visitors (volunteers, grandparents), puzzles, and manipulative play at art, reading, and special art project areas or sensory tables. This time is used for children to return to or extend projects they worked on previously in the day or week.
1:20–2:25 pm	Free choice play, project-based learning, or writing and creative projects Includes flexible grouping, emergent learning projects, and access to play areas.
2:35–2:45 pm	Closing routine Includes children's positive reflection, theme song, chant, poem, or other consistent ritual.
2:45–3 pm	Dismissal and family greeting

Figure 1.1. Sample schedules for half-day and full-day preschool programs to support a variety of child-centered teaching experiences.

NAEYC Standard 2—Curriculum provides practical help for planning a daily schedule. "The daily schedule must include both indoor and outdoor experiences, sufficient time and support for transitions, and periods of rest, active play, and learning experiences" (NAEYC 2018, 21). For preschoolers, "the schedule should provide time for creative expression, large and small group activities, and child-initiated activities. Some learning opportunities, experiences, or projects should extend over the course of several days" (21). Standard 2—Curriculum also requires that curriculum include adaptations and modifications to ensure access and to create individualized learning experiences for all children (NAEYC 2018).

Standard 3—Teaching states that teachers should "use their knowledge of individual children to modify strategies and materials to enhance an individual child's learning" (45).

REFLECTION QUESTIONS

1. As you review the scenarios from this chapter, what did teachers need to do ahead of time to make the activities successful?

2. After reading the information about developmentally appropriate practice and responsiveness to individual children, what would you like to change about your lesson planning to strengthen your interactions with children?

3. Describe two planning approaches that are highly effective for you. What two strategies would you like to adopt from this chapter that will have a positive impact on children?

CHAPTER 2

Making Lesson Planning Work for You

Ms. Ellie has read the book *The Jolly Postman or Other People's Letters*, by Janet and Allan Ahlberg, to the children. They enjoyed looking at the pictures in *Postman Pig and His Busy Neighbors*, by Richard Scarry. The children get ideas from the books about writing postcards for their families. Ms. Ellie supports learning by observing and asking questions. She encourages the boys to write a message on the back of the postcards. Having a real-life purpose for writing inspires the children.

In her lesson plan, Ms. Ellie includes a list of materials for the writing center. She adds the questions she wants to ask the children, such as "Where are you sending your card?," "What will you write in your message?," and "What letters do you need?" Her goal is for the children to understand the purpose of writing and to experience writing as a way to connect with people in their lives.

When programs focus heavily on standards or are more academically focused, it can be challenging to add child-centered questions and choices. Children learn best through hands-on, interactive experiences. In academically based programs, play experiences can be used to extend teacher-directed activities and content learning goals. The postcard activity builds on the children's reading experiences. Lesson planning helps you plan these extensions.

Engaging Children in Active Learning

Ms. Ellie sits next to the children in the writing center. She watches Jack and Nathan stamp letters on postcards. "Where are you sending your card?" Jack answers, "My uncle in Alabama. He has an alligator in his yard, so I made an alligator. He has sharp teeth." Nathan replies, "I made a cat. It's for my grandma." Ms. Ellie says, "You drew animals for your uncle and grandma." She watches Jack searching for letter stamps. "What letters do you need?"

A well-organized plan impacts teaching effectiveness in several ways. It helps you keep track of materials needed. It reminds you of the vocabulary to use in each play area. It keeps your focus on the big ideas you want to teach. A lesson plan helps you choose books, activities, and dramatic play activities that provide ongoing opportunities for children to practice skills. It will help you "get ahead" of your day-to-day needs and be more proactive in planning your setting and materials. A lesson plan ensures that you have prepared an effective context for learning.

Positive Communication with Children

In addition to carefully crafted lesson plans, a positive emotional climate is essential for social-emotional development and learning (McNally & Slutsky 2018). Healthy relationships with children ensure their psychological safety for learning. Positive relationships are the foundation for children's healthy development (Hall-Kenyon & Rosborough 2017).

Positive relationships with teachers have been referred to as therapeutic in supporting children's social and emotional development (Lindo et al. 2014). To be specific, "relationships characterized by sensitivity, attunement, consistency, trustworthiness, cognitive stimulation, and scaffolding enable children to develop secure attachments and mature in progressively complex ways" (Osher et al. 2020, 7). Positive, nurturing relationships with teachers help children achieve

> Stronger attention and impulse control, executive function, self-regulation, and problem-solving skills (Ertürk Kara, Gönen, & Pianta 2017)

> Increased ability to regulate stress, higher academic engagement, positive self-perceptions about learning, stronger pre-academic skills, and overall better academic and behavioral outcomes (Jones, Bub, & Raver 2013)

> Better adjustment and classroom behavior (Lippard et al. 2018)

> Increased capacity to overcome risk factors, manage adversity and trauma, and develop resilience (Osher et al. 2020)

> Enhanced capability to manage stress and develop resilience, self-efficacy, and self-regulation (Sciaraffa, Zeanah, & Zeanah 2018)

> Improved current and future academic success (McNally & Slutsky 2018)

Consider the following strategies to boost your connections with children:

> **Make conversation personal.** Learn about children. Ask about their ideas, feelings, and perspectives.

> **Talk one-on-one with each child daily.** Make sure children understand expectations. See if they need support. Watch for emerging skills. Use this information to plan activities.

> **Listen carefully.** Give eye contact and empathetic focus. Understanding children's experiences and needs is the first step to providing individualized support and encouragement.

> **Share positive experiences with families.** During pick up and drop off, share a strength or contribution each child made. Your daily affirmations will help children feel appreciated and valued.

> **Celebrate accomplishments.** Children thrive when given personal encouragement and positive support. Notice when children show pride in their work, satisfaction in a play experience, or joy at learning new information. These are strengths you can build on.

Planning a Variety of Teaching Contexts

During circle time, Ms. Malia asks the children to brainstorm what they do to care for their pets. The children have a lot to share: "I feed my goldfish," "I brush my dog," "I give my parakeet seeds and water," and "Mamma took my cat to the vet when she had kittens." Ms. Malia draws a large circle on the whiteboard. She makes sketches of a bird, a cat, a dog, and a fish inside. She draws lines outward and adds a leash, a bowl, water, and food at the end of the line that leads to the dog.

"What do you notice about the animals in the circle? Can they feed themselves like you do? Can they open the door to go outside?" The children giggle. "That's funny," says Adam. "They need us to feed them."

"That's right," says Ms. Malia. "What else do they need you to do?" "I let my dog out," says Adam. Ms. Malia extends his thinking. "You take responsibility for your dog. What do you think *responsibility* means?" Georgia says, "They can't do it by themselves. We have to do it for them." Adam adds, "They would be hungry."

Ms. Malia wants the children to understand the concept of responsibility. She begins by brainstorming the needs of pets. When the children offer their ideas, she writes what they say underneath the drawings: "Pets depend on us" and "We have to help."

Next, she asks how children take responsibility for their pets. She reintroduces responsibility during dramatic play, as children engage in pet care. She talks about responsibility for the environment when children water the plants. She reinforces the concept of responsibility as children put their things away after play. She knows they will remember when they encounter the idea in many ways.

Ms. Malia again talks about responsibility during lunch. She asks, "How do you help your families?" When the children answer, she says, "Ohhh, you are so responsible." She promotes the concept during fine motor play by giving feedback: "Thanks for taking on the responsibility of picking up the puzzle pieces on the floor." During the transition to outside play, Ms. Malia asks, "What do we need to be responsible for when we go outside?" The children respond that they need to help each other and be safe on the equipment.

When the children return from outdoor play, Ms. Malia reads *The Emperor's Egg*, by Martin Jenkins. The children are amazed at the responsibility the emperor penguin shows as he carries the egg on his feet in the cold. Ms. Malia places the book in the science area and pairs it with a cold water experiment. The children put their hands inside plastic bags filled with shortening before placing their hands in the icy water. This activity helps the children understand how the penguin could stay warm in cold weather.

Learning is multilayered, complex, and ongoing. Children learn while deeply absorbed in constructing a complex structure. They explore math concepts like size and spatial relationships; use position and shape vocabulary like *above, below*, and *rectangle*; practice social skills like negotiating and asking for help; and incorporate representational skills as they carry out ideas about building and replicating architecture. They learn new concepts and skills during dramatic play and while enjoying social games. These activities require self-regulation for planning and taking turns; organizational skills like following procedures and managing steps and materials; academic skills like counting, cardinality, and sequencing; and motor skills like balancing, manipulating, and coordinating the body. Planning ahead can help you support these skills throughout the day during activities, meals, routines, and transitions.

Creating a Rich Context for Learning

For young children, comprehension and engagement depend on context clues. They learn by connecting what they hear to what they see you do and to what is happening around them. Children rely on your tone of voice and gestures to understand new word meanings. When you ask them to do something, they notice what happens before and after your request. By observing your actions, they determine if your request is pressing, important, or casual. A rich context for learning helps them make meaning and deepens their understanding.

The following strategies will help you create a meaningful context for learning:

> **Prepare children for what comes next.** Children work best when routines are consistent from day to day. This helps them focus on learning and play without anxiety. When information is new, children need low-stress opportunities to figure things out.

> **Introduce information in multiple ways.** Adding real-life objects, illustrations, photos, sounds, videos, dramatic reenactment, or puppets can help children see ideas in different ways (Lessow-Hurley 2013). Storytelling, songs, and book reading reinforce concepts and help children make sense of new vocabulary (Espinosa 2018).

> **Introduce vocabulary in a variety of contexts.** Reinforcing a new word during play, lunch, and reading helps children remember and try out the word in their own conversation.

> **Include new vocabulary in home languages.** For children learning multiple languages, new vocabulary can be introduced in English along with the home language. It helps to make a connection between languages. For example, ask children, "How do you say *breakfast* in Spanish? *El desayuno. ¿Que comiste en el desayuno?* What did you have for breakfast?" These connections enrich the learning experience for all children, not just for those learning English.

> **Connect to what children know.** You may need to add or change information when you notice that children don't understand a concept you present. For example, a child may pause in the middle of a task, not sure what to do next. She may answer a question with an interesting insight that shows she has a similar idea, but doesn't grasp the actual meaning of a word. Perhaps a child repeats a mistake, rather than trying a new strategy or approach. While teaching, you can connect new concepts and skills to experiences children are familiar with in the classroom and in their lives. When you tap into funds of knowledge—that is, family strengths, values, and experiences—children are excited to learn (Sawyer et al. 2016). They learn more quickly and think, "Oh! It's like that! We do that too!"

> **Make new information specific.** When introducing new information, use clear, short sentences. Use repetition and paraphrasing (Echevarría, Vogt, & Short 2017. Show, as well as tell, what a word or concept means.

> **Follow up with feedback and positive support.** Talking with children about what they are doing and checking for understanding ensures comprehension (Cheatham, Jimenez-Silva, & Park 2015). Observe carefully to make sure children can use materials and tools to carry out an activity independently.

> **Group children in ways that make the most sense for their success.** Encourage cooperative activities to help children try new ideas without fear of failure. You may want to engage a whole group of children as they get started on a project. You may want to introduce new concepts or skills to a single child or a small group. Your grouping choices ensure support for language, learning, and social needs.

As you determine the best way to present new information, you will need to consider five important questions:

1. What are the goals for teaching and learning? In other words, what new skills or information do you want children to discover, learn, practice, or understand?

2. What methods of teaching and activities will provide the richest and most meaningful ways for children to reach those goals?

3. What teaching strategies will best engage children during the activity?

4. How will children demonstrate that they have mastered the skill, vocabulary, disposition, or competency?

5. What kind of documentation will capture children's learning?

All teaching with young children requires proactive planning for choosing strategies, activities, and grouping to fit the learning objectives. As you reflect on your teaching approaches, these questions can help you provide a rich context for the children you teach.

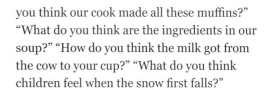

INDIVIDUALIZED TEACHING
Planning Personal Conversation

Preparing questions ahead of time can help you engage meaningfully with children throughout the day. Personal conversations boost learning, strengthen vocabulary, and encourage engagement with new ideas and thinking. See what happens when you ask the following questions:

› **What did you learn when . . . ?** During meals and care routines, ask children to tell you where they went with their family, what they enjoyed, and what they saw. Use the question "What did you learn?" in addition to "What did you do?" Children love to share their discoveries.

› **What (or how) do you think . . . ?** Ask these questions during transitions to outdoor play and during meals. You will find out what children know, experience, and feel. "How do you think our cook made all these muffins?" "What do you think are the ingredients in our soup?" "How do you think the milk got from the cow to your cup?" "What do you think children feel when the snow first falls?"

› **Guess what I saw?** Use "Guess what I saw?" prompts during daily routines. Tell children you saw six school buses in a row. You saw and heard a fire engine. You saw a building so tall you had to look straight up to see the top. You saw an entire flock of geese honking loudly. You saw a squirrel chasing a chipmunk. When you share "I spy" experiences, children will too.

› **Did you know . . . ?** When you know children enjoy a specific topic, take time during meals, dressing, nap preparation, and hand washing to share new information about that subject. "Did you know . . . ?" prompts make interactions fun and interesting. "Did you know a dog sleeps more hours every day than you do?" "Did you know cats can see in the dark?" "Did you know there are 27 bones in your hand and 26 bones in your foot? Hands have more bones than feet!"

› **How did it go? Tell me what happened.** When a family says a pet was taken to the veterinarian, be sure to follow up later and ask the child to tell you what happened. When you remember, children feel special.

Exploring Levels of Support in Child-Centered Teaching

Two children stack blocks and add a parking garage next to their skyscraper. There is a noisy debate about which side will connect to the street. Roberto insists, "There are lots of cars so the door has to go that way." Mr. Sanchez asks, "Will the blocks reach to the street? How many more blocks do you need?" Roberto looks at his drawing and then stares at the blocks. He says, "Maybe ten."

Mr. Sanchez asks, "Why do architects design tall buildings? Why can't the designs be flat and spread out?" Wanda answers, "There's not enough space." "That's right," says Mr. Sanchez. "The architect creates buildings that go up to use the space in the air instead of on the ground."

The children explore a variety of books about architects, skyscrapers, bridges, and famous buildings. Mr. Sanchez takes them to a nearby city park to compare the differences and similarities between surrounding buildings. The investigation provides information for their classroom building decisions. Mr. Sanchez asks questions to help the children think about their choices.

A child-centered classroom provides a combination of teacher leading and children leading for different parts of the day. Teachers evaluate the goals for learning and the most effective options for activities, materials, and supports for the particular children. The successful engagement of children during a lesson about architects may seem effortless, but the activities and teaching strategies are selected with a purpose.

To make lesson planning effective, it helps to define teaching as *the level and type of support provided by teachers in response to the needs of children*. In this way, child-centered teaching can be examined on a continuum, rather than through the lens of separate or distinct approaches. This integrated connection creates a useful balance or bridge between child-directed playful learning and teacher-directed learning (Hassinger-Das, Hirsh-Pasek, & Golinkoff 2017).

Child-centered teaching requires flexible levels of support that shift from teacher-directed to child-centered *in response to the individual needs of children*. This responsive approach facilitates development and learning in ways that meet learning goals while ensuring sensitivity to children. You will adjust your level of support to facilitate the greatest possible engagement, comfort, and competence for children.

Understanding the framework for each type of teaching strategy will make lesson planning more effective:

> In child-discovery learning, you plan and use strategies to foster independent, solitary, or focused collaborative play.

> In child-directed learning, you plan and use strategies to facilitate and enrich children's interactive play.

> In shared learning, you plan and use strategies to guide emergent curriculum. Emergent curriculum develops in response to children's interests, such as exploring informational books and introducing hands-on activities to answer questions. It can include carrying out simple or complex project-based investigations that focus on real-life topics.

> In teacher-guided learning, you plan and use strategies to lead mini-lessons and introduce group activities, skills, or games.

> In teacher-directed learning, you plan and use strategies for direct instruction; model concepts using stories, conversations, pictures, and demonstrations; and introduce new ideas and more complex skills using hands-on materials, learning games, and activities.

The following section explores how each of the above approaches can support the specific goals of learning and the needs of children. Each vignette is followed by a set of questions designed to clarify what is happening in the narrative. Questions include: What are children doing? What are teachers doing? What does the approach look like? When does it work best? How does it impact lesson planning? In each type of teaching, both the teacher and children take active roles in participation and learning. Guidance includes how to design and facilitate each kind of learning.

Supporting Child-Discovery Learning

At the nature table, the children reach into wooden bowls that hold knobbed sticks, sweet gum balls, and sugar maple spinner seeds. Pinecones, tree bark, branch "cookies," and dried flowers are stored in baskets within reach. A clear plastic container holds a variety of shells. Soft white sand is spread in individual shallow trays. The children press and roll the objects into the sand to make patterns. They use tiny rakes and miniature shovels to draw patterns.

It is very quiet, except for Robert, who is humming. Sylvia gets up to retrieve a spray water bottle. She wets her shells and presses them into the sand tray. Next to her, Robert stacks the small branch cookies and creates a tiny walkway in a circular pattern around the border. He balances pinecones on the top ledge of each cookie and occasionally reaches for another stick or seed pod.

Ms. Eileen watches with interest. She stands a few feet away so she doesn't interrupt the children's concentration. When a pod rolls off the table, she picks it up and hands it to Robert. "Thanks," he says and adds, "I'm making a forest house." She responds. "When you are finished, we can take a picture."

What are children doing? Discovery learning takes place during independent, solitary, or collaborative work or play when children are deeply absorbed. In discovery learning, children are active explorers. They play with minimal intervention from adults except when needed to ensure safety or well-being.

What are teachers doing? In child-discovery learning, teachers are active observers. While play appears to be "independent," teachers have carefully prepared the setting and materials. They remain near to notice and record children's activities. Over time, they adjust materials to match children's choices, ideas, and interests. They use their understanding of children's developmental skills to organize the spaces and materials.

What does it look like? Examples of child-discovery learning include loose parts play, creative art projects, exploration of natural objects and collections, fine motor play, sand and water play, and block play. When children are deeply engaged in these activities, teacher intervention may distract from imaginative or creative concentration. Children are absorbed and need time to think deeply, figure out problems, and experiment with materials in their own way.

When does it work best? Child-discovery learning is effective in the context of consistent routines when children know what is expected. The environment must be well prepared to match the stimulation needs of children. In addition, teachers must be sensitive to children's level of productivity and engagement. Child-discovery learning is an appropriate choice when interference or conversation would interrupt or undermine a child's focus, self-directed concentration, or independent productive play.

How does it impact lesson planning? In child-discovery lesson planning, teachers evaluate the developmental and learning needs of individual children. They choose and arrange materials to facilitate emerging skills. With this level of support, they plan spaces to invite prolonged engagement and exploration with an appropriate level of challenge.

Facilitating Child-Directed Learning

> In the housekeeping area, Esther sighs dramatically. "Ohhh, my back aches. Honey, you hold the baby." She dumps the baby doll onto Twyla's lap. "Give her a bottle. I'm making dinner." Twyla makes the baby burp loudly. "Good baby. You gotta big burp."
>
> George bumps into the table with a stroller. "I'm going shopping." He uses a clipboard with a pen attached. "What's on the list?" he asks Twyla. She says, "Get chocolate milk." Esther says, "Get pumpkin pie." George scribbles busily. Esther adds, "Buy diapers."
>
> Ms. Sami hands George a wallet. "Here you go, George. Be sure to count the money before you go. Tell Esther and Twyla if you think there is enough money for the chocolate milk, pumpkin pie, and diapers."

What are children doing? Child-directed learning takes place during a variety of play activities. In child-directed learning, children are active designers. They explore and play in well-prepared settings. They initiate, choose, and direct the flow of activities. The term *guided play* is also used to describe this kind of play, in which teachers prepare objects and materials intentionally to promote learning with clear goals in mind (Hirsh-Pasek et al. 2008). The purpose is to provide opportunities for children to engage with concepts, vocabulary, and new ideas.

What are teachers doing? While child-directed play and learning appear "natural," there is a high degree of preparation. Teachers know children well and evaluate moment-by-moment opportunities to facilitate learning. They support without taking over or interrupting the flow of activities or the intention of children. They may initiate conversations to prompt greater complexity in children's thinking. They may support problem solving by asking questions.

This level of support requires clear understanding of learning goals, along with deep knowledge of children's emerging skills and competencies.

What does it look like? Child-directed learning takes place when children are involved in dramatic play and free-choice activities at learning or activity centers. Teachers ask questions to challenge their thinking. They may introduce more challenging props and show children how to use them. These gentle interventions help children make connections between their play, thinking, and ideas (Blake 2009). Guided play helps children solve problems, persist through challenges, build vocabulary skills, and gain background knowledge.

When does it work best? To be effective, teachers must have a high degree of understanding of individual children. They must plan spaces and materials for easy accessibility and appropriate stimulation. They are careful observers and watch for opportunities to introduce vocabulary and questions to prompt higher-level thinking. Children must be familiar with the routines and expectations.

How does it impact lesson planning? In child-directed lesson planning, teachers embed specific goals for learning. They choose materials and activities that facilitate these goals. They select books that engage children in reading and extend concepts into play activities. They identify a list of vocabulary that supports learning goals and prepare related questions and prompts. While teachers have an intentional plan, they remain responsive to children's questions, interests, and needs.

Shared Learning for Emergent Curriculum

> "Look at the bee!" Marissa points excitedly. "Let's make an investigation of why bees are in the sandbox." Josh says, "Look at his antennae. That's how they get their prey." Marissa adds, "When they crawl inside a flower, they hang upside down and attach their stinger." Josh says, "I saw the bee, but he didn't think I was his enemy. He

went back to the flower. Why does it go upside down in the flower?" Ms. Jaana answers, "Let's look at the insect book and see if we can find an answer."

Shared learning or emergent curriculum can have different meanings, depending on your approach and philosophy. An important concept of emergent curriculum is the idea that children respond to their environments with a mindset of curiosity and expanding ideas about their world in guided explorations with their teacher (Fleer 2010). Activities build on and expand children's understanding by helping them investigate their interests and ideas. Children's interests are visible when they return to the same books or play themes or ask questions about specific topics during indoor and outdoor play. Some emergent projects are brief and may be completed in a day or two. More in-depth projects, sometimes called *project-based learning,* can involve explorations that take place over a few weeks or even a few months. Many teachers use the terms *project-based learning* and *emergent curriculum* interchangeably.

What are children doing? Children are interested in patterns, events, and problems they encounter in daily life. They are eager to explore topics of interest in more depth. Children learn to collect, organize, and present information using written and oral communication. Their findings often generate additional ideas and questions.

What is the teacher doing? Emergent curriculum follows children's lead, yet requires the full participation and guidance of adults who observe, listen, document children's questions, and extend learning. Teachers provide additional materials and situations to facilitate ongoing learning. Children explore and test their ideas, explain their thinking and receive feedback, elaborate and extend what they know, and evaluate learning by demonstrating what they know (Rodriguez et al. 2019).

What does it look like? An important part of emergent curriculum is asking open-ended questions that engage children's thinking processes (Nunamaker, Mosier, & Pickett 2017). Guiding questions help children explore how and why events happened. Teachers help children notice details and ask why these are present. They make connections to what children already know. Teachers guide children to ask, "I wonder how (if, why) this happens?"

When does it work best? As children seek more information about a topic, teachers may provide informational books, invite guest speakers, arrange field trips, or provide tools and resources for exploration. For example, children will need bug containers, magnifying glasses, and science journals to engage in an insect study. They can watch a video about recycling before sorting materials. They can use a spider map to draw their ideas or use shoe boxes to organize materials. These supports help organize children's questions and the information they gather, and then help children draw conclusions about their findings (Watt et al. 2013).

How does it impact lesson planning? Play experiences introduce many opportunities to guide emergent learning (Trundle & Smith 2017). Classroom activities and materials can be selected to help children explore issues or solve problems. Lesson planning can

› Expand on children's knowledge about their current interests as they notice relationships, events, and experiences around them

› Help children make connections across areas of content learning. For example, when children are exploring weather patterns or caring for pets, they are also learning to communicate, organize information, use math knowledge, and apply creative skills.

› Support a variety of skill levels, including the contributions of all children's prior experiences

› Embed IEP goals and other individualized learning supports

Exploring Emergent Curriculum

Emergent curriculum is a flexible and important approach to learning in all kinds of early childhood programs. No matter your teaching philosophy or approach, and even with time restraints, you can include emergent curriculum in a variety of ways.

Emergent learning takes place during brief, teachable moments as you capitalize on children's interests and questions. A teacher may spend a few minutes looking more deeply at something the child has seen or look up information in a book to show the child how to find the answer to a question. The children may compare different insects collected outside and determine how they move.

Emergent learning may include a short-term project for children to explore their interests. You may prepare children for a field trip. A classroom visitor can introduce children to ideas, materials, or stories to learn more about a topic. You may delve more deeply into something children experience, like a changing season or what it feels like to move to a new school. A school or local librarian can provide a variety of informational books that focus on a theme or topic.

Emergent learning also can involve longer, more in-depth projects that take place over weeks or months as children explore ideas, problems, and solutions. For example, you may spend six weeks exploring how plants grow. You will engage students in planting seeds, experimenting with different sources of light, and comparing watering schedules. You may hatch tadpoles and investigate the life cycle of a frog. You can explore types of artwork, like collages, mobiles, or weaving. The idea is to provide time, information, and materials for children to learn in depth.

While there are many examples of emergent curriculum and project-based learning available, the guiding principle is to *follow the interests of the specific children you teach*. Help them extend their curiosity and build on the wonder they show about your unique setting. Children in New England may study the changing seasons. Children in Arizona may study how cactuses grow. Children in Wyoming may explore how the wind moves objects. You'll find that children have many ideas and questions about their own world. The following resources provide more information:

> Emergent Curriculum (NAEYC topic page): NAEYC.org/resources/topics/emergent-curriculum

> "Implementing the Project Approach in an Inclusive Classroom: A Teacher's First Attempt with Project-Based Learning," by Stacey Alfonso (*Voices of Practitioners* article): NAEYC.org/resources/pubs/yc/mar2017/project-approach-inclusive-classroom

> "Inspired by Reggio Emilia: Emergent Curriculum in Relationship-Driven Learning Environments," by Mary Ann Biermeier (*Young Children* article): NAEYC.org/resources/pubs/yc/nov2015/emergent-curriculum

> Project Approach (NAEYC topic page): NAEYC.org/resources/topics/project-approach

> The Project Approach (website providing examples of successful projects for prekindergarten and kindergarten children): www.projectapproach.org/project-examples/pre-k-kindergarten

> Science (NAEYC topic page): NAEYC.org/resources/topics/science

Strengthening Teacher-Guided Learning

> In the science area, Megan and Thea pull apart pinecone scales and watch the seeds drop onto the table. They peer at the seeds through magnifying glasses. They count the seeds and place them in small plastic tubes. They want to see which cone has the most seeds. Megan says, "I shook my seeds out."
>
> Mr. Sanchez asks, "What do you notice? How will the seeds fall out of the pinecones if you don't shake them out?" Thea responds, "Maybe when the pinecones hit the ground, the seeds fall out." Megan says, "Maybe the rain gets them out." Mr. Sanchez introduces a book that illustrates how birds, animals, and the wind carry seeds to other places.

What are children doing? Children are active partners in engagement but follow the teacher's lead. Children continue to have a high degree of autonomy and choice. They participate in hands-on experiences with many materials. They ask questions and participate in meaningful conversations.

What is the teacher doing? In teacher-guided learning, teachers introduce and model specific skills. They may plan a brief mini-lesson that adds a higher or deeper level of complexity or demonstrates new skills. Whether carried out one-on-one or in small groups, there is a set purpose for the modeling and support. Teachers connect the new skills or knowledge to what children already know. They remain responsive to support emerging competence.

What does it look like? In teacher-guided learning, teachers work with children individually or in flexible, small groups to demonstrate and scaffold learning. It can take place during mini-lessons or adult-facilitated group activities. Adults prepare materials and activities and provide modeling to introduce new skills or information.

This strategy is used during math games, big body play, science experiments, and other learning games and activities that require new knowledge, skills,

or procedures. Teachers may introduce a new song, read to children, or engage them in activities with a specific goal.

When does it work best? Teacher-guided learning is appropriate when children have just begun to learn skills or use materials, such as building ramps to roll balls or working with tangrams. This is a preferred strategy during reading and writing workshops. It is used whenever teacher modeling and verbal support are needed to introduce new ideas, vocabulary, or skills. To be successful, teachers must demonstrate a high level of responsiveness, strong personal relationships, and respect for individual development and learning needs.

How does it impact lesson planning? In teacher-guided lesson planning, a specific introduction and scaffolding are planned. Typically, activities at this level are brief, skill specific, engaging for children, and designed to meet a particular learning goal. Activities facilitate children's development. Alternate information, materials, and approaches are used to meet the needs of children at various skill levels.

Enriching Teacher-Directed Learning (Direct Instruction)

> Ms. Blaire has just finished reading *The Rainbow Fish*, by Marcus Pfister. She highlights the words, *sparkling*, *shimmer*, and *dazzling*. She pulls a box forward and takes out a soft rag and a spray bottle of water. She sprays a hand mirror and wipes it dry. Peering into the mirror, she says, "Hmm. This mirror is *shiny*." The children giggle. "Let's see. What else do I have in my silvery box that is shiny?"
>
> Ms. Blaire takes out a silverware spoon, a brass key, a patent leather shoe, and sunglasses. She puts them next to a wooden spoon, a sponge, a tennis shoe, and a rubber ball. "Which of these is shiny and which of these is dull?" The children say, "The mirror is shiny. The key is shiny." Martin says, "One shoe is dull, and one shoe is shiny."

Shuntae says, "My daddy says I am a shining star." Ms. Blair says, "Sometimes people use descriptive words like 'shining star' to show how they feel. You are like a shining star."

Teacher-directed learning, sometimes called *direct instruction,* takes place during modeling of new skills and introduction of new concepts. Teacher-directed learning is used to introduce targeted knowledge, skills, vocabulary, or concepts. This approach is used during individual support and in small or large group experiences.

What are children doing? Children may be asked to work with the teacher or in a group, observe teacher modeling, or answer specific questions. Children are active partners in engagement but follow the teacher's lead.

What is the teacher doing? The teacher may introduce skills in brief mini-lessons that are followed by individual or small group activities. Teachers may assign roles and invite engagement in prescribed ways—that is, ways that require children to follow directions, take sequenced steps, or compete specific tasks. Teachers use real-life objects and illustrations and ask questions to engage children.

What does it look like? Teacher-directed learning takes place in mini-lessons related to content learning, such as book reading, a gross motor game, a music activity, math or science learning, or a social studies experience. Other examples include a morning circle with elements of a song and movement, a morning greeting, daily social sharing, or instructions that prepare children for the day.

When does it work best? Appropriate teacher-directed learning minimizes rote activities and maximizes opportunities for children to learn from each other, participate actively, and respond to open-ended questions. Teacher-directed approaches must be flexible and responsive to the needs of children. For example, a teacher may shorten an activity when she notices children need a movement break. She may add materials when she realizes children do not understand a concept as she has presented it. Monitoring children's engagement and sensitivity to their needs is required.

How does it impact lesson planning?
At this level of support, learning goals with targeted skills are identified. Teachers plan materials and prioritize the vocabulary and concepts they want to model, introduce, or strengthen. They plan specific connections to children's background knowledge and experiences. They adapt and extend materials and support to meet the needs of specific children. Planning includes questions, prompts, cues, and opportunities for children to interact with materials to ensure engagement and interest.

TIPS FOR TEACHING

Effective Strategies to Support Child-Centered Learning

Rather than plan only for what children will be doing, child-centered lesson planning offers an organized blueprint for you to prepare *what you will be doing* to support a specific group of children and a specific type of learning. As you review Table 2.1, keep in mind that the purpose for a continuum of teaching strategies is to help you decide what you need to do *ahead of time,* what you need to do *during* teaching times, and what you need to do *after* teaching times. Without this perspective, you may find that you prepare only what you need to do ahead of time!

Teaching strategies may be used in succession—meaning first one approach and then another. For example, you may want to start an activity with teacher-guided strategies, giving explicit instructions and modeling how to interact with materials. Then you will move the children forward to engage in child-directed learning.

For the teacher-guided instructions in your lesson plan, you can

⟩ Write the steps for your introduction.

⟩ Make bullet points to remind yourself of what you want to ask and say.

⟩ List the materials needed for your mini-lesson.

⟩ Describe how you will walk children through the steps of a game or activity.

Continuum of Teaching Strategies		
Type of Strategy	**Role of the Teacher**	**When to Use It?**
Child-Discovery Learning Children are: Active explorers	Prepare the setting, actively observe and document, and ensure appropriate challenge. Intervene when safety or frustration are present.	During exploration, imaginative play, building, construction, task-oriented play.
Child-Directed Learning Children are: Active designers	Prepare the setting, scaffold and support learning, stimulate emerging skills, increase complexity and challenge, introduce and extend concepts, and enhance vocabulary.	During dramatic play and manipulative or exploratory play.
Shared Learning for Emergent Curriculum Children are: Collaborative learners	Document questions, provide processes and resources, and support demonstration of new knowledge.	During teaching moments, short-term projects, or longer-term investigations.
Teacher-Guided Learning Children are: Active participants	Introduce skills, strategies and concepts, demonstrate and scaffold learning, and facilitate cooperative activities.	During new activities and with new concepts or materials.
Teacher-Directed Learning Children are: Active learners	Teach and model new skills, and lead or facilitate mini-lessons, games, or small and large group interactive activities.	During content mini-lessons, reading, math games, and math talk.

Table 2.1

When children are able to play the game or carry out the activity independently, this then becomes child-directed learning. Next in your lesson plan, you can

> Write the purpose for learning.

> List the materials children need.

> Highlight the vocabulary, questions, and concepts you want to support.

> Describe how you will document what children learn.

It's up to you to evaluate the situation and the needs of the children and the purpose of the learning *before* you start teaching—to be sure you are ready to go. Instead of "figuring things out" as you go along, you will have a plan of action that provides essential structure and purpose to the flow of the experience—for you and for the children.

With a lesson plan, you can evaluate the sequence of events, materials, concepts, vocabulary, or strategies you need to introduce ahead of time. Within each context, you can challenge thinking, boost knowledge, and adjust materials for the greatest impact. This makes your teaching proactive.

Perhaps you are planning to promote child-discovery learning. In that case, you need to consider whether children will have enough space, whether they will be distracted, and whether the materials are adequately challenging. You'll need to be sure the materials alone provide interesting play possibilities for curious hands and minds. You may want to prepare items that offer a greater level of challenge. Lesson planning can help you become more effective in all learning situations.

Adding Teaching Strategies to Lesson Planning

As you plan for teaching, what choices will you offer children? How will you engage them in meaningful conversation? What materials will provide hands-on experiences? Whatever strategies you choose, children need to be active agents in their own learning.

In playful learning, children are active participants in achieving academic objectives (Stipek 2017). Your role is to promote higher-level thinking. You will challenge children to engage with real-life problems and use hands-on teaching tools. Across the continuum of teaching strategies, continue to be responsive to individual children.

When you develop specific lesson plans, don't try to add everything at once. Choose a part that feels "doable" for your approach and setting. You will explore examples of child-discovery, child-guided, and emergent learning in Chapter 3. You will explore examples of teacher-guided and teacher-directed learning in Chapter 4. You can start with one strategy at a time.

For **child-discovery learning**, describe the activity. Include learning goals and target skills (what will children need to manage and do?). Provide a list of materials. Add individual adaptations, extensions, and supports to ensure children are successful. Determine how to document and evaluate children's learning.

For **child-guided learning**, describe the activity. Include learning goals, target skills, and a list of materials. List vocabulary, concepts, and questions to prompt thinking and understanding. Add individual adaptations, extensions, and supports to ensure children are appropriately challenged. Determine how to document and evaluate children's learning.

For **emergent curriculum**, record children's questions for inquiry or project-based learning. Create a plan to locate information and monitor children's progress. Add individual adaptations, extensions, and supports to ensure children are successful. Help children choose a way to demonstrate learning.

For **teacher-guided learning**, describe the activity. Include learning goals, target skills, and a list of materials. List vocabulary, concepts, and questions to prompt thinking and understanding. Add individual adaptations, extensions, and supports to ensure children are successful. Determine how to document and evaluate children's learning.

For **teacher-directed learning**, describe the activity. Include learning goals, target skills, and materials. List vocabulary, concepts, and questions to prompt thinking and understanding. Add individual adaptations, extensions, and supports to ensure children are successful. Determine how to document and evaluate children's learning.

Each of these approaches

> Can be linked to early learning guidelines, NAEYC Early Learning Program Accreditation Standards, and state preschool standards to choose essential goals and objectives for learning

> Requires a child-centered understanding of observation, documentation, and assessment (see Chapter 5)

> Requires reflection to consider what went well, to determine what you want to do differently next time, and to explore what you learned about children and the impact of your strategies

Being Consistent While Staying Flexible

The children are making playdough donuts for their bakery. Joshua and Maggy reach for the baker's apron at the same time and pull on it. Ms. Celeste says, "I see you both want the apron. Is there another one?" Joshua says, "Here's one in the basket."

Ms. Celeste moves their attention forward. "It's important for bakers to wear an apron so customers know who will help them. What are other reasons a baker wears an apron?" Joshua answers, "So they don't get chocolate on their clothes." "So they don't get sticky," adds Maggy.

Ms. Celeste notices the brief struggle with the apron and gently narrates what she sees. She quickly shifts the focus to talk about the purpose of wearing an apron. With caring guidance, the children reengage easily in bakery play.

This dramatic play theme began with donuts children made earlier in the week. They painted designs on the dried clay. The children created menus by drawing pictures and writing prices. A local bakery donated the hats. Ms. Celeste used flour-sack towels for aprons. A parent screwed knobs to the shelf to create ovens with "temperature controls." Families donated pans and containers. This activity required detailed preparation.

Bakker (2018) emphasizes that "the paradox is that the more autonomy we want to give students, the better we have to design the task" (173). Each strategy for supporting learning requires active planning and responsiveness. In addition to the activity itself, you must be ready to assist children as they transition in and out of the activity. You'll help children solve problems when challenges are present. How do children interact with materials? Is it what you expected? You'll need to make ongoing adjustments to conversations, materials, and levels of scaffolding to ensure an activity goes well!

As you become deeply attuned to children, you will develop sensitivity to their cues and needs. Your approaches to teaching will become aligned with the ways they learn. You will adjust your level of support to encourage autonomy, choice, and confidence as they develop skills. Your sensitivity to individual children will become the favorite tool in your teaching toolbox. With detailed lesson planning, you will have an accurate set of instructions to guide effective teaching.

TIPS FOR TEACHING

Getting Organized and Staying Inspired

Take small steps. Try one new strategy at a time. See how children respond. Then add on to the materials and strategies you use. Small steps lead to big impact.

Set aside a dedicated time each week to prepare. Add lesson planning to your weekly and monthly calendar. You'll get on top of the sequence of planning by dedicating time. You will be able to schedule time to prepare materials, find or borrow books, and arrange spaces. This will minimize last-minute preparation.

Keep a reflection journal. At the end of each day, enter a brief description to document what you discovered about yourself, what you learned about children, or a bright idea that worked well. Answer two simple prompts: "What did I do and how did it turn out?" and "What did I observe and what did I learn?" Your answers will help you recognize the incredible influence you have in teaching.

Talk to colleagues. When teaching goes well, share your experience. When you need fresh ideas or support to overcome a challenge, reach out and connect. You and your colleagues can grow together.

RESEARCH CONNECTIONS

Increasing Opportunities for Learning

Robert Pianta and colleagues (2018) describe three essential ingredients of learning for the preschool classroom: (1) teacher practices and child engagement, (2) classroom activities and settings, and (3) children's exposure to instructional content. They studied 117 preschool classrooms and found (similar to past findings) that among these classrooms, about 40 percent of the observed school day was spent in teacher-directed activities, with 28 percent of time in whole group, 6 percent in small group, and 4 percent in individualized interactions. With 40 percent of time focused on teacher-directed instruction, the remainder of the day was split between free play (30 percent) and meals, routines, and transitions (30 percent).

The researchers wanted to know what children were learning during these activities and transitions. During the total day, about 35 percent of time involved teachers supporting academic learning, with a focus on literacy and social studies. Within teacher support, only 4 percent of time was focused on social-emotional learning. Teachers taught basic skills; however, more analytically focused instruction was rare, accounting for about 3 percent of the time. About half the day was spent in managerial instruction and general conversation.

Field Note: Making Minor Changes with Major Impact

The children hardly touched the baby dolls. Most of the time, the dolls were upside down in a pile in the baby crib. My coteacher and I cut colored socks to make knit caps for the dolls. Then we rolled up hand towels in the same bright colors to make sleeping bags. We made a tent with inexpensive mosquito netting suspended from a wall hook. We tied simple bandanas around the stuffed animals and added cardboard "binoculars." Afterward, I read *Henry and Mudge and the Starry Night,* by Cynthia Rylant, at reading time. The children made up camping stories for two weeks! And they learned about forest wildlife and the big dipper.

These findings reveal that without intentional planning and focus, it's hard to get ahead of basic routines and basic skills. The authors discuss the following priorities (Pianta et al. 2018):

> Managing time in ways that intentionally promote learning for children *throughout the day*

> Consistently focusing on teaching language, self-regulation, and social skills during routines and meals, as well as other activities

> Engaging children in critical thinking skills, like categorizing objects based on characteristics, brainstorming, and higher-level exploration of concepts

Intentional planning can ensure all children experience a wide variety of rich and adequately challenging learning opportunities throughout each day. Detailed lesson planning can help you evaluate the way you use your time and design experiences that enrich and strengthen children's learning and development.

HELPFUL HINT

Planning Materials for Play

When planning materials and props for play, think about what kinds of experiences will engage children in more complex learning. The idea is to put together a collection of thematic accessories, props, and costumes that help children reenact events from their daily lives. Good sources of content are stories and characters from books, including informational picture books that introduce new concepts and ideas.

After determining a thematic goal, store and organize materials in clear tubs or containers. A full range of accessories can be kept together so you can keep track of inventory. For example, keep an item list taped to the lid of each container so you can see what is included. Include a "Next Time" sheet to jot down reminders for what worked well and what you would like to do next time to introduce vocabulary, books, or additional props.

Build out your themes with a variety of supportive props. You may have coats and stethoscopes for health care workers, but add a doctor's pad, wrap bandages, doctor bags, a cot, and a telephone. Slip in books like *Dr. Meow's Big Emergency,* by Sam Lloyd, and *The Berenstain Bears Go to the Doctor,* by Stan and Jan Berenstain. Use your own creative ideas to think about enriching play, such as using wall displays, adding mosquito netting, or building a hospital with boxes. The children will eagerly engage.

For teacher play, add a lap-sized chalk- or whiteboard, several ABC books, pencils, stickers, papers, tape, backpacks, and a bell. Include books such as *Teachers,* by Cari Meister, and *The Night Before Preschool,* by Natasha Wing. Ask children what they want added. They will have many practical and doable ideas to enrich their play.

Sample Lesson Plans

Planning Thematic Play Experiences

For lesson planning, the themes and related objectives you choose will be consistent with high-quality, achievable, and challenging early learning standards (NAEYC 2018). You will discover how to use these in Chapter 3. You'll prepare a unit or theme for teaching based on children's specific interests or curriculum topics. Planning content often starts with the big ideas. Other times, a simple question or idea can inspire a larger theme.

Use graphic organizers like those featured in Figure 2.1 to record questions or ideas that support exploration of a larger theme. Alternately, begin with a larger theme idea and brainstorm more specific ideas and concepts that you can to build out into activities and play experiences.

When developing a theme, it often helps to start with a list of books, as these introduce ideas about characters, concepts, and vocabulary. You may brainstorm a list of materials and consider how to relate the new ideas to children's lives. As you plan, you will discover many creative ideas to support children's engagement.

Sometimes, programs or districts provide suggested lesson plans. These documents can be used as a starting point for individualized planning. Each teacher must know children well and make decisions that support their specific development and learning needs. Teaching choices and strategies must be responsive to the diversities of children and their families, including languages, cultures, social experiences, and community contexts. Materials, activities, and spaces must reflect the lives of the children. Activities planned for the beginning of a year will not provide appropriate challenge, rigor, and stimulation over time. Spaces, materials, and teaching strategies must be reviewed continually to ensure these are relevant for the group and for individual children.

The example in Figure 2.2 illustrates what can be planned to support child-discovery and child-directed learning through an architecture and construction theme. It provides ten introductory books, materials, concepts and vocabulary, questions to inspire learning, and integrated activities.

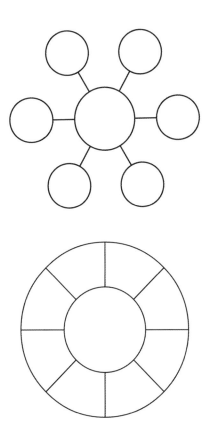

Figure 2.1. Examples of graphic organizers to record ideas for exploring themes while planning content.

This book shows a variety of sample themes, including animals, families, health and nutrition, housekeeping, recycling, social-emotional learning, travel, and weather. There are limitless possibilities, but the samples illustrate how to think about themes in a holistic way. Over time, all areas of learning and development will be supported and strengthened. You'll consider what can make each learning experience real, meaningful, relevant to children's lives, and engaging.

In the following chapters, you'll see how big ideas and concepts can be integrated fully across play areas and interest centers. You will discover how to identify the many skills that children need to be successful as they learn. You'll become more comfortable making needed modifications and adaptations to ensure full engagement and success. You'll explore many strategies to ensure learning has taken place through authentic assessment.

Plans Following an Architecture and Construction Theme

Early Learning Standards

> Presentation of knowledge and ideas: SL.PK.5
Use drawings or visual displays to add to description to provide additional detail.

> Conventions of standard English: L.PK.1e
Use frequently occurring prepositions
(e.g., *to*, *from*, *in*, *out*, *on*, *off*, for, *by*, *with*).

> Initiative, engagement, and persistence: 9.1.5
Bring a teacher-directed or self-initiated task, activity, or project to completion.

> Applying learning new situations: 9.4.1
Use prior knowledge to understand new experiences or a problem in a new context.

> Mathematics

- 4.4.1 Respond to and use positional words
(e.g., *in*, *under*, *between*, *down*, *behind*).

- 4.42 Use accurate terms to name and describe some two-dimensional shapes and begin to use accurate terms to name and describe some three-dimensional shapes (e.g., *circle*, *square*, *triangle*, *sphere*, *cylinder*, *cube*, *side point*, *angle*).

(Standards Include From New Jersey Department of Education 2014 Preschool Teaching and Learning)

Concepts and Big Ideas

Children will engage with materials, books, and conversation to understand that:

> People build places to live, work, and help their community (e.g., fire houses, hospitals, libraries, schools, playgrounds).

> People build with materials (e.g., bricks, wood, stones, glass).

> People design and draw plans before they build.

> People design to fit a specific space and purpose (e.g., skyscrapers; low, flat buildings; barns; ship and airplane hangars).

> People cooperate with others (e.g., plumbers, brick layers, glass installers, and electricians) to complete a building project.

> Architects design to fit the setting.

> Construction workers need plans and tools to build.

> Buildings are designed with a purpose (e.g., houses, fire station, doctor's office, apartment building, bakery)

Reading Library: Architecture and Construction Books

> *Billions of Bricks*, by Kurt Cyrus

> *Build It from A to Z*, by Trish Holland

> *Building a House*, by Byron Barton

> *Construction Workers*, by Cari Meister

> *Construction Workers Help*, by Tami Deedrick

> *Iggy Peck*, Architect, by Andrea Beaty

> *Jack the Builder*, by Stuart J. Murphy

> *Look at that Building: A First Book of Structures*, by Scot Richie

> *Made by Maxine*, by Ruth Spiro

> *Rosie Revere, Engineer*, by Andrea Beaty

> *Same, Same but Different*, by Jenny Sue Kostecki-Shaw

> *What Can You Do with a Toolbox?* by Anthony Carrino and John Colaneri

Academic Vocabulary

> *balance, compare, connect, construct, design, install, measure, plan, predict, trace, solve*

Content Vocabulary

> *base, beam, ceiling, column, design, feature, foundation, horizontal, materials, replicate, space, square, structure, triangle, vertical, wall*; position words (*between, next to, over, under*)

Thought Questions and Prompts

> Tell me about your design.

> What do you need to do first, next, last?

> Who will use your building?

> What features will you design?

> What tools do you need to use?

> How does that work?

> What community workers will help you?

> What do you think? What do you think will happen?

> How will you make it fit? (balance, taller, larger, smaller)

> What will you do next?

> How can you solve that problem?

> What will go over, under, next to, between?

Integrated Activities

> **Reading and language:** See book list.

> **Phonemic awareness and phonics:** *C* says "K" as in construction, classroom, community, connect, cap, cart, color, compare.

> **Dramatic play:** Construction worker vests, tools, tool boxes or belts, helmets, safety glasses, maps, safety tape, retractable measuring tapes, gloves, signs, and a clipboard with graph paper, rulers, pencils, camera.

> **Mathematics/fine motor:** Measure items in the classroom with measuring tapes. Sequencing puzzles by attribute of length and height. Memory game with laminated pictures of bulldozer, concrete mixer, dump truck, forklift, grader, excavator, tools, hat.

> **Science/nature:** Exploring natural construction materials (sand, pebbles, stones, rocks, wood, glass, silk) made by animals, from the earth, and from plants.

> **Social skills/self-regulation:** Solving problems. (1) What's the problem? (2) What's a good solution? (Try it.) (3) Did it work?

> **Sand and water:** Smooth ramps, pipes, scoops, shovels, cups, dump trucks, conveyer belts, Lincoln logs, smooth black pebbles, builders' levels.

> **Visual arts:** Painting buildings using easel and our town wall mural sketches of buildings; making mosaic buildings with tissue paper, fabric, and sewing accessories.

> **Music and movement:** Song "This is the way we pound a nail (saw the wood, drill a hole, use a screwdriver) early in the morning."

Figure 2.2. Plans following an architecture and construction theme. (Standards from New Jersey State Department of Education [2014].)

NAEYC Standard 2—Curriculum asks teachers to focus on a comprehensive curriculum that explores all areas of learning: social, emotional, physical, language, and cognitive development. Content areas for learning include literacy, mathematics, science, technology, social studies, health and safety, and creative expression, and appreciation of the arts. Importantly, "the curriculum should allow for the development of a daily schedule that is predictable, yet flexible and responsive to the individual children's needs" (NAEYC 2018, 21).

The NAEYC standards provide the rationale and purposes for specific teaching practices. Whatever the content material or goals of learning, curriculum should be "implemented in a way that reflects the family values, beliefs, experiences, cultures, and languages of all enrolled children" (21). This means that you will continually reconsider the best ways to introduce information, provide teaching support, and encourage play and learning activities.

As you review the recommended practices in the content areas, you will find specific explanations for what children need to know and understand, and how they can best learn it. You will find information presented from the child's point of view and be able to reflect on the ways you create a safe and secure learning setting.

Standard 3—Teaching provides an important rationale for lesson planning. Teaching staff should "purposefully use multiple instructional approaches [to] optimize children's opportunities for learning. These approaches include strategies that range from structured to unstructured and from adult directed to child directed" (NAEYC 2018, 40).

Predictable but flexible routines include many ways of interacting with materials, peers, and adults. Teachers provide adequate structure yet remain responsive to the needs of children throughout the day.

Standard 3.B focuses on creating a caring community, one in which "teachers develop individual relationships with children by providing care that is responsive, attentive, consistent, comforting, supportive, and culturally sensitive" (41). This mandate applies to supervision, decision making, making learning meaningful, and practicing a mindset of reflection, to ensure you are continually growing and learning more about teaching practices.

Standard 3.F ensures that learning is meaningful for all children. "Learning is most effective when it is relevant to each child's life" (45).

Standard 4D.4 ensures that program management gives teachers collaborative planning time at least weekly.

Standard 6A.7 ensures that written program policies include information about staff planning time.

REFLECTION QUESTIONS

As you build on your current approaches to planning, consider small steps you want to take and new strategies you want to use. Take time to answer the following questions:

1. What part of your current lesson planning is working well?

2. What would you like to change or improve?

3. What new learning themes would you like to introduce? What kinds of play props and collections would support that theme?

4. As you think about the scenarios and sequence of teaching approaches introduced in this chapter, what new teaching strategies would you like to use?

5. What specific development and learning skills would you like children to know and be able to do? What books, props, interactions, and activities will strengthen those skills?

CHAPTER 3

Preparing Child-Centered Themes and Play Areas

focus to keep the rubber bands where they belong." Eisley says, "My rubber band flied away too." Ms. Kristina says, "Yes, your rubber band flew off too."

As the children begin, Ms. Kristina demonstrates a completed geoboard. She shows the children how to press board patterns over the pegs. She helps them turn the geoboard so that the pattern is right side up. She also demonstrates how to roll the band down to the bottom of the pegs so it won't slip off. She includes several sizes of geoboards so children can choose what works best. Planning ahead makes this activity successful.

As children select rubber bands and slip them over the pegs of a geoboard, they practice multiple skills. They need fine motor coordination to handle the paper patterns, slip them over the pegs, and manipulate the rubber bands. They use decision making as they choose patterns. They compare and contrast as they select rubber bands by color and size. They use persistence as they work diligently. They use executive function as they avoid external distractions to finish a pattern. They use communication skills to request help from a peer or a teacher. This analytical perspective—the ability to identify the skills children must have to be successful completing an activity—is a critical part of lesson planning. You'll need to plan the purpose of an activity, identify the skills required, and understand the context of learning.

Identifying Learning Goals for Play

Greyson and Eisley are working intently. They select rubber bands and bend forward to slide them over the geoboard pegs. Greyson's rubber band flies off and lands on Eisley's arm. Ms. Kristina steps over to reassure Eisley. "Greyson is working on the side of the barn pattern. The rubber band flew away like a bird. Are you okay?" Eisley nods. Ms. Kristina adds, "It takes a lot of

Before planning a play area and deciding which objects for exploration, activities, books, or materials to include, it's important to know the purpose. Rather than ask what children will be doing, a learning goal answers the question, "What will children be learning as they engage in this activity or with these materials?"

Learning Goals Relate to Content

Learning goals include cognitive development, language acquisition and vocabulary development for single and dual language learners, gross and fine motor development, social-emotional development, and content areas like science, math, social studies, and literacy. Once you identify learning goals, you'll be able to plan the activity as well as the level and type of teaching support needed to reach those goals. The following questions will help connect learning goals to the way you plan for play:

> What early learning guidelines and content area concepts do you want children to explore when they use specific props, materials, spaces, and ways of playing?

> What big ideas (concepts) will children be learning?

> What specific materials and activities will best support the learning goal? What will children be exploring, discovering, trying, reenacting, or solving?

> What vocabulary and concepts need to be introduced and explained?

> What guiding questions will promote thinking skills? What questions will children ask?

Learning Goals Relate to Skills

As you plan play spaces and specific materials, identify the skills required.

> What skills will children need to participate successfully? Will they need to be able to see, hear, and communicate? Will they use fine motor skills to manipulate objects? Will they need to solve social problems and manage their emotions? Will they need self-regulation skills to plan, cooperate, and organize their play?

> What will children be able to do independently? What parts of the activity will need your support? How will children be able to assist each other?

> What emerging skills will this activity strengthen? Are there a range of challenges present to meet the needs of individual children?

Learning Goals Relate to Context

As you plan play activities and materials, consider what children already know and understand.

> What background knowledge will help children understand the purpose or procedures?

> What patterns and connections (similarities, differences, and links) will children make to experiences that are already familiar and important to them?

> What materials will motivate creativity, critical thinking, and engagement about culture, family, and neighborhood experiences?

Learning Goals Relate to Standards

Learning goals correspond with state or curriculum's early learning and development goals, guidelines, or standards. Children practice these skills with teachers and peers during block play, dramatic play, and fine and gross motor play.

The following are examples of learning goals:

> **Physical goal.** Children will stack blocks and use words to describe their actions.

> **Language goal.** Children will identify objects in book illustrations in response to teacher questions and retell events in the story.

> **Cognitive/learning goal.** Children will use simple maps to identify and represent familiar locations and landmarks.

> **Personal development goal.** Children will carry out classroom routines with independence (e.g., hang up coat, clean up toys).

> **Social-emotional/language goal.** Children will use words to describe emotions.

With a clear purpose or learning goal, you will be able to identify the types of materials, activities, and interactions that will advance the goal. For example, when you want to teach children about responsibility, what experiences will support that goal? Here are some ideas:

> Select and read picture books that depict children taking care of pets and helping families.

> Organize the housekeeping area with stuffed animals and pet care items like leashes, bowls, and brushes to encourage pet care.

> Create a mural that displays photographs of children helping their families at home.

> Ask children to describe what they do at home to help their families.

> Invite children to tell stories about helping their friends.

> Notice and narrate when you see children showing helping behaviors in the classroom.

By identifying learning goals first, you can make clear choices for lesson planning and identify children's progress toward these goals. You'll be better able to evaluate what to do to teach new skills, strengthen emerging skills, and add complexity to advancing skills.

Field Note: Designing Something to Learn Versus Something to Do

I used to create play centers to give children something to do. I followed a list of materials I got from my program. Then I asked the question, "What are children learning?" It opened my eyes to why they got bored and wanted what the other children had. So I made my first dramatic play prop box. Then I made another. Finally, I could rotate materials based on a specific book or theme. I am still adding to and changing materials to update the boxes. Now the props and costumes are ready when needed and give children everything they need to get absorbed in play.

Recognizing Interdependence Among Areas of Development and Learning

Easton and Hannah are hard at work at the fine motor table. Easton makes a pattern using brightly colored tiles. Ms. Hazel says, "Tell me about the pattern." Easton answers. "I have two red squares and three yellow triangles.

Ms. Hazel asks, "Where are the red squares?" Easton points. "Where are the triangles?" Easton points again. Ms. Hazel asks, "What shapes will you add next?" Easton answers, "Next come four blue squares." "That's great," Ms. Hazel responds. "You have a repeating pattern."

Hannah says, "I have red, yellow, and blue. Red, yellow, and blue are the color of my dress." "You are right," says Ms. Hazel. "Clothes designers make patterns that repeat in fabrics. You have the same color pattern in your dress."

The children have recently celebrated a Polish American festival in their city. Ms. Hazel added costumes with flower and ribbon hats for dress up and dancing. She added color tiles and pattern designs to the fine motor table. Her lesson plans for the week focus on patterns and comparing. These concepts are extended to the play areas of the classroom.

At the science center, children line up objects from smallest to largest. They sort bean pods to see which is longer and shorter. In the math area, children weigh vehicles to decide which is heavier or lighter. At the sensory table, children roll playdough with a variety of pasta rollers to compare straight, wavy, and zigzag patterns. At the sand and water table, children use tubes with narrow to thick diameters to compare the quantities of sand and water that emerge through funnels. In the art area, children make collages with bright scraps of paper, fabric, and ribbon. By integrating themes across the play areas, Ms. Hazel has many opportunities to talk with children about patterns, colors, sorting, and comparing.

Ms. Hazel knows that play boosts children's communication and language skills, including listening, talking, and explaining ideas. Successful play involves executive function skills, such as attending, shifting attention, planning, monitoring tasks, and carrying out plans. Children learn to recognize and respect the feelings of self and others, manage frustrations, and communicate their needs. Play strengthens social skills that help children participate successfully with others.

During dramatic play, children use math skills to set the table and decide how many items are needed. They count as they play with money and use menus, signs, and games. They use measuring during construction, sand table, and cooking activities. Math is linked to community workers through projects and measuring tools. Math in daily life is vital as they count number of lunches, children present, and steps needed to go outside. Math is represented in books, pictures, and displays. These multiple experiences form layers of support for learning.

Math skills are also present in science, technology, engineering, art, and math (STEAM) activities through culturally inclusive imaginative play with open-ended materials and learning projects (Broughton & McClary 2019/2020). Children learn sequencing during fine motor games like tangrams, peg sorting, design cards, child-generated designs, and jigsaw puzzles. Pattern blocks, puzzles, and shape games build math skills during fine motor activities, whereas dramatic and art activities promote math learning during creative play (Mixon 2015; Reed & Mercer Young 2018).

Problem solving is strengthened through construction with materials like LEGO bricks and Magna-Tiles. Children use math vocabulary like *how many*, *add*, and *take away* as they play with blocks. Board and card games reinforce one-to-one correspondence, addition, and subtraction skills. Hands-on math manipulatives help children represent grouping, adding, and taking away objects.

During play, children combine or integrate skills to accomplish a goal. For example, to pretend to go shopping during dramatic play, children need self-regulation to pay attention, organize steps, and coordinate choices with peers. They use language skills to ask for items and fine motor skills to create a shopping list on a clipboard. It is important to identify these skills ahead of time and consider what kind of space, materials, and supports children will need to be successful.

Transforming Teaching

Supporting Emerging Skills and Dispositions

Mr. George has modified a Chutes and Ladders type game by creating a path for caterpillars to travel on a laminated file folder. Sally and Elias roll two cubes to tell them how many spaces to move their pieces along the board. At the end of the game, the goal is a colorful chrysalis, where the caterpillars can become butterflies. Along the way are leaves and twigs for the caterpillars to "eat" as they travel along the path.

"My caterpillar went faster than yours. He went eight squares," Elias insists. Sally says, "I'm going to roll a double six, so I can go past you. That's the most." Mr. George intervenes. He turns the cubes over until the children can see both with six dots. "This is the most . . . six plus six. Let's count them together to make twelve."

The adapted board game with counting cubes reinforces the stable order of numbers, one-to-one correspondence, and cardinality, which means that the last number counted represents the total number of the group. The cubes include the written number with dots to show "how many." Sally is able to subitize, or recognize the quantity just by looking at the dots. She counts up from three dots on one cube to add on two more from the second cube. Elias needs to point to each dot on both cubes to figure out the total number. When Mr. George shows them the sum of two sixes, he reinforces the concept of two equal numbers. Board games give the children a real math workout (Moomaw 2015). This game meets the needs of both children at different levels of understanding.

In addition, playful classroom learning supports qualities like persistence, effort, creativity, and problem-solving skills, which are predictors of future school success (Neuenschwander et al. 2012). Children learn to negotiate, collaborate, and work toward mutual goals. Playful learning contributes to these needed dispositions, skills, and competencies (Moreno, Shwayder, & Friedman 2017).

As you plan child-centered activities, you'll engage children in a way that fits their learning needs. How well do you know each child? Can you describe each child's emerging skills? Do you regularly observe and document what they are doing? Do you capture their learning through written notes, photographs, videos, and samples of their work? Do you know what motivates and excites them about learning?

As you plan activities, consider the attitudes, skills, and approaches to learning that are important. The following questions will help you consider the impact of your plans:

> What parts of the lesson or play experience will teach critical thinking and problem solving?

> How will children need to work together? How will you foster collaboration?

> How can you help children think in new ways about their work and the possibilities for learning?

> What books or materials might lead to ongoing investigation and inspiration for learning?

> What will inspire curiosity, creativity, and imagination about this topic in children's play?

> What vocabulary will children need to understand the concepts being explored and to share their ideas?

> What part of the activity will introduce children to each other's perspectives and ideas?

As you become more attuned to children's flexibility, collaboration, problem solving, and engagement, adapt your support or adjust materials when you see children need additional challenges. The more you know about children's emerging skills and capabilities, the more you can be responsive in preparing experiences that match their needs.

Exploring Standards and Early Learning Guidelines

State departments of education provide links to important birth-to-5 resources, such as early learning guidelines and resources for working with children from culturally and linguistically diverse families. Early learning guidelines present the content children encounter during the pre-K year. The more you understand the concepts and vocabulary associated with each area of learning, the more effective you will be in planning lessons. This knowledge helps to identify the best approach to teaching—child-discovery learning, child-directed learning, shared learning, teacher-guided learning, or teacher-directed learning—to provide integrated layers of support for learning. (See Chapter 2 for a thorough description of the different approaches to teaching.)

In addition to descriptions of the content areas, state departments of education also offer suggestions for teaching practice. Visit the US Department of Education's State Contacts page to locate your own state's resources: www2.ed.gov/about/contacts/state/index.html.

Digging Deeper with Content Skills for Child-Centered Teaching

Emmett and Jordyn huddle inside a cardboard box canoe with a flashlight and explore the book *If I Ran the Rain Forest*, by Bonnie Worth. "There's not really children in the rainforest talking to animals. That's pretend," says Jordyn. Emmett agrees, "Yeah, but the hummingbirds and parrots are real." Ms. Penny says, "You are both right. Jordyn says there aren't really children in the rainforest talking to

animals. Emmett says there really are hummingbirds and parrots. Sometimes real and make-believe characters are in books at the same time. Jordyn, you found something make-believe, and Emmett, you found something real."

Ms. Penny's classroom looks like a rainforest. Crumpled brown paper bags create tree trunks, with large green leaves hanging over the reading area. The children have created toucans, scarlet macaws, and birds of paradise with paper tubes, paint, and feathers. The brightly colored birds bob from the green palm leaves. A small, kente-design hammock shelf holds books about rainforest animals: chameleons, red-eyed tree frogs, monkeys, sloths, lemurs, anteaters, and orangutans. The wall of the reading area is covered with the children's paintings and drawings of these animals. The children read in boxes that have been fastened together as canoes. There is a big sign hanging above them. It says, "The Amazon River."

The math area introduces math games and puzzles using rainforest animals, like a toucan counting game and monkey jigsaw puzzles. Ms. Penny created the puzzles by adhering color-prints of animals from the *National Geographic* website onto cardboard and cutting them into puzzle pieces.

The children are learning about rainforest layers. They brainstorm homes they want to live in, like tree houses and tents with suspended bridges. They create a mural that wraps around the room and shows the different kinds of trees and flowers. They hang their forest drawings on the mural. Ms. Penny plays ambient rainforest sounds as the children get ready for afternoon napping. They listen to the birds, water, and other nature sounds of the rainforest.

In the midst of this setting, Ms. Penny has written lesson plans to address each area of content learning. She knows that when learning relates to real-life experiences, children are motivated and engaged. She knows this child-centered space, where children can explore and choose activities freely, will engage children in exploration of new ideas and materials. She has specific learning goals for each area that are based on state pre-K level content guidelines.

Skills Development

Content learning is supported by children's physical, social-emotional, and self-regulatory skills and by their communication, language, and literacy development. Take a closer look.

Physical development. During the pre-K year, children develop increasingly complex motor skills that support other areas of development (Battaglia et al. 2019). In addition to fine and gross motor coordination, curriculum includes nutrition, health and well-being, and management of stress and trauma (Bartlett & Steber 2019). Children gain competence in self-management, personal care, and hygiene as they practice healthy physical habits. They take on increasing responsibility as they show concern for others as well as themselves.

Social-emotional development. Children need to be able to identify and respond appropriately to the cues of others and manage their own emotions. They need to coordinate plans, communicate about their feelings, and regulate emotions in social situations (Campbell et al. 2016). Children learn to negotiate conflict, solve problems, and collaborate with others—skills essential for academic learning and behavior adjustment.

Self-regulation. Self-regulation includes a range of behaviors in which children can choose to control their actions, emotions, and attention (Rademacher & Koglin 2019). Children make active choices about their behaviors by using executive function. *Executive function* is a group of skills that includes children's ability to remember and use information, shift attention as needed, and activate or inhibit (delay or stop) behaviors to meet the needs of learning and social situations (Center on the Developing Child, n.d.). The development of executive function overlaps with language, cognitive, and physical maturity as children coordinate their skills to remember directions, control their bodies, and communicate their needs (Montroy et al. 2016). Children develop executive function and self-regulation with the support of caring adults who model positive behaviors and provide support for managing emotions and stress.

Communication, language, and literacy.
Language and literacy skills develop rapidly during the preschool years and require a specialized teaching (Skibbe et al. 2016). Multilingual language learners, as well, benefit from language-rich environments that build on the linguistic and cultural strengths of children's families (Kim & Plotka 2016). Foundational communication, language, and literacy skills include

> Recognizing symbols, labels, and signs in environmental print, books, and labels

> Internalizing the conventions of spoken English, including the forms of words, how to ask questions, the parts of speech, and the use of sentence forms

> Developing phonemic awareness, which includes recognizing and producing the similarities and differences in word sounds

> Understanding phonetic awareness, which includes knowing that written letters represent spoken sounds and that letters combine to make words

> Using new vocabulary to retell stories and share ideas and feelings

> Exploring emerging writing skills, including letter-sound correspondence, managing motor movements, and creating meaning (Gerde et al. 2019)

> Developing comfort with spoken language and listening skills to participate in social play and learning experiences

Children learn and practice these skills through word games, rhyming, sound patterning, identifying letter sounds, and blending and segmenting words. They explore books and practice language and literacy skills during dramatic play (Bluiett 2018). As adults write dictated stories and captions, children learn about the many real-life purposes of written words as communication. Communication, language, and literacy provide a strong foundation for content learning.

Content Areas

Content learning during pre-K occurs through exploration, meaningful conversations, indoor and outdoor play experiences, and exposure to daily life at school and at home. Math concepts depend on children's understanding of math language. Science and math are integrated as children count and compare natural objects and discuss events. With support, children begin to integrate the study of science, technology, engineering, the arts, and mathematics (STEAM). Physical health is integrated with science and nutrition. Processes of inquiry and problem solving are integrated across learning areas to foster meaningful connections and deepen children's understanding. While presented as separate areas, content is integrated multiple ways like Ms. Penny's rainforest study. Below are just some of the content concepts explored in the pre-K year.

Mathematics concepts. Children incorporate math concepts throughout the day. As they play and explore, children begin to

> Associate spoken numbers with the idea of "one" or "more than one"

> Learn one-to-one correspondence, cardinality (which number comes first or second, and so on), and sequencing (which number comes before and after)

> Sequence objects by size, color, shape, and other attributes

> Identify patterns, compare shapes, and use math language to do things like explain how many sides make a square or discuss whether one group has more or fewer objects than another

> Develop understanding of spatial relationships and position words (such as *over, under, up, down,* and *next to*)

> Represent numbers using objects, drawings, graphs, pictures, and symbols

> Compare ideas about quantities, collect data, and talk about their findings

Children learn these skills by talking about math in daily life, as they set the table or record the number of birds that come to a feeder. They enjoy counting books and playing card and board games. They practice sorting, matching, measuring, and comparing at sand and water tables. They enjoy solving simple story problems and using math for practical purposes while cooking, measuring, and counting money.

Science concepts. The study of nature and science depends on observations of events, cycles, and experiences in the real world. Children ask what, when, where, why, and how questions as they develop an understanding about patterns and concepts. They make predictions, gather evidence, explore ideas, and interpret information. They represent their thinking in pictures, graphics, charts, and symbols.

In the classroom, they use science tools like magnifying glasses, prisms, magnets, child-safe test tubes and containers, and tweezers to explore how things work and learn about cause and effect. They use simple machines, such as ramps, pulleys, and gears, to explore the impact of force and motion. Ramps and pathways teach children about angles, incline, weight, and gravity. They learn about technology used in daily life. They enjoy nature, as well as explore the need to take responsibility for protecting plants, animals, and the environment.

Social studies concepts. Children are curious about the similarities and differences in people, places, and events. They develop awareness of themselves within the context of multiple social identities. They enjoy representing their experiences through stories, play, and art. They discover that things change over time.

As children play, they begin to see the perspectives, strengths, and contributions of others. They learn the principles of democratic participation, including roles, rights, and responsibilities in the classroom. They also begin to appreciate and value differences and similarities among cultures, community experiences, and ways of communicating.

Visual arts, music, drama, and movement. Children participate in a rich variety of creative arts experiences as personal, creative, cultural, and social expression. They enjoy exploring art materials and processes. They identify and take pride in the classroom setting when they see their works displayed and represented in the environment. They engage in group musical activities and learn about a variety of forms and genres of music, dramatic, and creative arts. They sing, dance, play instruments, and make up

songs. The collaborative interaction and opportunities for self-expression inspire their aesthetic development and appreciation for creativity.

Fine motor, logic, and construction skills. Children learn to build complex block structures using physical, mental, and representational skills. They make patterns, create symmetry, explore balance, and produce increasingly complex designs. Block, logic, and construction play increase their creativity, problem solving, communication, and collaboration. These skills prepare children for future success in school and in the workplace.

Typically, more than one subject area or skill must be addressed at a time. If you want children to answer questions related to mathematics but don't realize they will need to cooperate with others, use tools, and follow steps to do so, you may not prepare the children or model what is needed. For example, to be successful, you may need to show children how to use a tool, provide enough space, or include a picture or anchor chart of the steps needed in an activity. To create effective lesson plans, you'll need to identify *all* the skills you want to teach.

HELPFUL HINT

Considering the What, How, and Where of Play Areas

In addition to planning materials, you'll need to plan the classroom setup. Do you have enough low shelving so children can find and use materials easily? Do you have groups of thematic props so children can reenact meaningful scenarios and imaginative play? Make sure children can find and navigate furniture, shelving, and materials with ease.

As you plan, take a look at spaces to be sure there is enough room for the type of play that will happen there. Children in the block area need to be able to spread out to build complex structures without running out of floor space. Children in housekeeping tend to be active and spread out to move around. Place these areas away from quiet play areas so noise and activity do not disturb other children. Protect spaces for quiet activities, such as reading and fine motor play.

Finally, watch carefully to be sure a variety of challenges are present. You'll know you have the right difficulty level when children engage for extended periods of time without interruption or frustration. By monitoring materials, spaces, and levels of challenge, you will see more consistent focus and satisfaction.

RESEARCH CONNECTIONS

Creating Active Learners

Children are curious and dynamic learners. During the preschool year, they develop critical skills called *approaches to learning*. These include

› Making purposeful choices and planning specific goals (McDermott, Rikoon, & Fantuzzo 2014)

› Pursuing challenges and persisting through problems (Bustamante & Hindman 2019)

› Being active agents—taking responsibility for—their own learning and seeing themselves as capable learners (Boylan, Barblett, & Knaus 2018)

› Developing critical thinking, problem solving, and negotiation skills (Chatzipanteli, Grammatikopoulos, & Gregoriadis 2014)

› Making choices and decisions during meaningful activities and hands-on learning (Hughes et al. 2017)

Haimovitz and Dwenk (2017) present strategies to support a growth mindset and help children develop dispositions for learning, such as effort and persistence. They suggest

› Focusing on children's effort and progress

› Connecting processes for learning to positive outcomes

- Talking about strategies that are not effective and those that work well

- Talking through ways to solve problems

- Modeling strategies and ways to use materials

- Encouraging children to take risks and try increasingly challenging tasks

- Letting children know adults and peers will support learning

- Ensuring high expectations for all children

Fostering Language Development During Play

Ms. Julie sits on a low stool. She says, "Let's see if you can do what I do." She claps her hands slowly three times. The children repeat her motions. She taps her knees quickly in a pattern, "Rat-a-tat-tat." With some laughter, the children do it too. Ms. Julie puts her hands on her hips and tightens her face into a scowl. The children laugh and make the same face.

Ms. Julie says, "You are imitating me! Joel, now you make a body pattern, and we will copy you." Joel stamps his feet on the floor and then pats his head. The children do it too. Ms. Julie says, "Some people say, 'Monkey see, monkey do.' That means that people—and monkeys—have fun copying each other's actions. We do this when we play follow the leader."

Skye says, "My baby sister imitates me when I laugh." Ms. Julie smiles. "Yes. Children and babies have fun when they imitate each other. In the story we're about to read, you'll see how the monkeys imitate the man by putting caps on their heads."

Ms. Julie has a goal to accomplish before she begins reading the book *Caps for Sale*, by Esphyr Slobodkina. In addition to teaching the concept of *imitation*, she needs the children to notice and understand that the man in the book stacks and balances the caps on his head. She prepares a stack of eight caps. She shows how placing one on top of the other creates a stack. She adds the caps to the dramatic play area, so that after they finish the story, the children can reenact the actions of the characters.

TIPS FOR TEACHING

Maximizing Language Support

Preschool teachers often do not engage with children using explicit, intentional language modeling (Phillips, Zhao, & Weekley 2018). This area of teaching is critical because language competency is the foundation for reading and other learning experiences. Below are some high-impact language strategies to enrich teaching, play, routines, and meal activities:

- **Build on what children know.** Children reenact what they know, such as visiting the market, going to the bakery, taking the subway in the city, or observing farming activities in a rural area.

- **Introduce vocabulary.** Use a vocabulary list to remind you to use specific words in conversation with children. For example, during fine motor, logic (e.g., puzzles, games, manipulatives), and construction activities, you can include math concept words like *first, second, third, same, different, less, more, large, bigger, smaller, all,* and *none*. Position words include *above, below, beside, behind, in front, back, inside, next to,* and *outside*. Descriptive words include *open, closed, balanced, centered, tall, short,* and *bridge*. Shape words include *square,* circle, triangle, cube, cylinder, and tube. Write vocabulary words on an index card to use as a reminder during the children's play activities.

> **Use specific language.** Instead of saying, "Put that over there," say, "Hang your red scarf on the hook." Instead of "You can play with that if you want," say, "You and Joshua can choose the giraffe puzzle or the lion puzzle." The goal is to use specific and descriptive words for people, places, things, and actions. "Green beans are vegetables that are cooked. Cucumbers and carrots are not cooked. Cucumbers and carrots are vegetables too. Can you name vegetables that we cook?"

> **Introduce advanced vocabulary.** Use specific descriptive words for objects, events, and emotions. "It feels breezy. *Breezy* is another word for windy." "The purple flowers are African violets. The leaves are fuzzy and curled. Let's give them some water." "A group of cows is called a *herd*. Young cows are heifers and young bulls are bull calves."

> **Use back-and-forth exchanges.** "I want to paint." "Let's get a new paper and fresh water. What are you thinking about painting?" "I want to make a picture of my family." "Who is at home?" "My sisters, grandma, and my dog."

> **Scaffold thinking.** Use verbal mapping to describe what children are doing or what you are doing. "I think if I move the puzzle over, the rest of the pieces won't fall off the table." "I see you organized your scale and blocks before you got started. That will make your work easier."

> **Add on information.** When a child says, "I saw a fuzzy worm," use this as a teaching moment and elaborate. "You saw a brown caterpillar with yellow stripes. It looks like a fuzzy worm, but a caterpillar has a soft, hairy body with lots of legs. Do you see the legs? A caterpillar will spin a cocoon called a chrysalis and become a butterfly."

> **Ask open-ended questions.** Ask how, why, what if, and what else questions to encourage children to explain, predict, and consider new concepts. "How will the pilots refuel when it is raining outside?" "What tools do the explorers need to dig for treasure?" "What problems do you notice?" "How did you (they) make that happen?" "Why do you think she feels sad?"

> **Notice and narrate children's actions, strategies, and experiences.** Often called *parallel talk*, narrating children's actions or experiences draws attention to strategies that work well. Narrating children's feelings helps them notice and respond with productive solutions. "You asked for help when Declan took your car. Let's get the basket of cars so he can have one." "You look sad. Would you like to choose a book to read with me?" "I see you are feeling frustrated. Tell me about what you need."

> **Describe what children see.** "Are you watching the squirrel? Do you see its nest? Look higher to the left. Do you see the big clump of leaves? What do you notice about the leaves? They are thick. They are packed into the tree branches. The squirrels scamper in to hide."

> **Encourage book reading.** Add informational books with realistic drawings and photographs that depict topics of children's interest to boost planning and conversation.

> **Create a print-rich setting.** Include labels for play areas, materials, and props. Label spaces and clear containers where materials are stored. Include labels and captions in children's home languages as well as English.

HELPFUL HINT

Making Play More Complex

Extensions from a group activity into play don't need to be extraordinary, but they do need to be complete. This means that needed costumes, props, and materials are present to engage multiple children in a complex play theme. When plenty of materials are grouped together, children can reenact the concepts and experiences they learn about in teacher-directed activities and book reading. Here are two examples:

> If you have a conductor's hat, be sure to add a ticket book, a money pouch, a map, and a bell. Line up and attach cardboard boxes, so children have a "train." Read *The Little Train*, by Lois Lenski, with these props, and you'll see wonderful things happening.

> If you have a cash register, you'll need money and a money pouch. Add reusable shopping bags for multiple children. Collect small (empty) grocery items from home and tape the lids shut. Arrange them on a shelf to recreate a realistic "store." Add a scale so the children can weigh produce. Add bakery items on top of the display box with a tablecloth and small brown bags. Provide a baker's hat for the baker. Add baby strollers so families can shop together. Don't forget shopping lists. Include books like *What Happens at a Supermarket?* by Amy Hutchings. It will be easy for children to imagine they are at the market.

BALANCE POINTS

Planning Effective Behavior Guidance During Play

The goal of behavior guidance is to build children's skills. Children do the best they can in group settings as they manage transitions, change, and expectations. When they struggle, it's important to look at what's happening in the classroom that impacts their reaction.

Add notes to your daily lesson plans to remind you of positive redirection strategies. Explore *101 Principles for Positive Guidance: Creating Responsive Teachers* (Kersey & Masterson 2013).

Consider the whole child and his or her need for soothing from stress, consistent security and safety, and a meaningful personal relationship with you. Ensure routines are the same each day so that each child feels confident about what will happen next and knows how to do it.

In each interaction with you and others, assisting children to experience success in the moment will show them what skills work and how to handle a challenge. Add notes to your lesson plans for specific children. For example, "Get Wendy started at the sand table" and "Give instructions for the board game." Here are some other tips:

> **Review rules and procedures before children begin an activity or play experience.** "When you are in housekeeping, notice that the pans are under the stove and the plates are in the cupboard. There are new grocery items on the shelf for the store." "When you begin building with blocks, notice where the other children are around you. Make sure to give yourself enough space."

> **Validate feelings and brainstorm strategies.** "I see you are frustrated. Let's brainstorm a solution." "That looks challenging. What can we do to fix it?" Brainstorming helps children feel confident when trying new choices.

> **Encourage children to ask for and give help.** "Sometimes it's hard to get a puzzle started. When you get stuck, ask a teacher for help." "If you want to read with a teacher, raise your hand so we know to come." "If you need something, ask, 'Please may I have . . . ?'" "Look for ways to help others. Ask them, 'Do you need help?'"

> **Notice when children use effective strategies.** This approach is especially important for children whose social skills are still developing. Recognize and highlight great choices. "You stopped your hands from touching his bear. Good for you for steering your hands!" "Thank you for helping her carry the books. That was kind."

> **Move children forward.** Talk about what works and what the child can do next rather than what a child did that was ineffective. For example, "Let's put the dinosaurs on the table so you can play without getting interrupted." (Rather than, "You are in the way of other

children," or "Don't play on the floor.") Your goal is to make every interaction result in a positive outcome by giving support for the child's success. Through your verbal modeling and positive support, children learn how to solve problems.

Look for ways to redirect and reengage rather than focus on misbehavior. Don't wait until a pattern develops. The first time something doesn't work well, evaluate what you can adjust or adapt, such as preparing children differently, arranging materials in a new way, or modifying the length of an activity.

Providing a Rich Context for Multilingual Learning

> "I saw two black squirrels. They were chasing me!" Efrem says excitedly. "They scared me when they got by my feet." Braydon replies, "I had a moth knocking on my window, and it scared me." Jordie says, "I wasn't scared. I saw ants on the sidewalk. They didn't look up." Mr. Jasper smiles. "You all are noticing a lot of animals. Let's add them to our list."

Many of the children in Mr. Jasper's class live in high-rise apartments, and they don't often play outside. Their school is also in the city. In spite of the sidewalks, buildings, and cement parking lots that surround them, Mr. Jasper wants them to develop a love for nature and to notice the diversity of plants and animals in the neighborhood. In the classroom is an aquarium and a plastic box with a hermit crab, and just outside the window are two bird feeders. He encourages children to help care for the animals. Next to the window in the science area, there are paper cups sprouting seeds, and a tangle of potted plants.

Mr. Jasper challenges the children to generate a list of all the plants and animals they see on the way to school. The children bring in leaves, branches, pinecones, and weeds. They begin to identify birds and talk excitedly about the animals they have spotted. When the children bring in objects, they are added to the natural collections. Braydon found a

bird's nest of great interest to the others. A basket of books about nature includes *Caterpillars, Bugs, and Butterflies* and *Birds, Nests, and Eggs*, both by Mel Boring; *Trees, Leaves, and Bark,* by Diane Burns; and *On the Nature Trail,* by Storey Publishing. Mr. Jasper helps the children look up the treasured items in these books.

The following strategies help learning come alive and connect to the children's lives and interests. These approaches make teaching meaningful and inspire learning.

Introduce concepts in multiple ways. When you teach children who are from different backgrounds or speak different languages, provide multiple ways to introduce new objects, concepts, and vocabulary. Using real-life examples that connect to what children already know helps build new knowledge. Try new strategies to introduce new vocabulary and concepts, such as the following:

> List objects that demonstrate the concept or word. In a group context, ask children to sort objects into categories.

> Label new objects in the children's home languages as well as in English.

> Connect new vocabulary and concepts to those children already know.

> Illustrate the meaning of words and concepts in multiple ways, such as acting out a word meaning and using real objects to demonstrate.

> Create an illustrated anchor chart for similar words and ask children to add to the list.

> Introduce the words and concepts during play and follow-up reading and activities.

> Read multiple books that demonstrate the same ideas, concepts, and vocabulary.

> Use a layered approach so children encounter concepts and vocabulary multiple times. Place objects and books used during small or large group activities into play areas for additional exploration. Revisit concepts and skills to provide additional exposure.

Separate and teach new academic language.
Recognizing the difference between informal, conversational English and academic vocabulary will help you be intentional about teaching new words. Academic language tends to be complex, like giving instructions or explaining procedures and processes. For example, *predict, figure out*, and *solve* are processes that need to be demonstrated. Academic language gives a lot of information at once, is complex, includes metaphors and figurative language, has a narrative structure, and uses content vocabulary (Luna 2017). To demonstrate the meaning of academic language, be sure to

> Use visual context clues, like nonverbal physical gestures and modeling.

> Connect new vocabulary to similar words children know.

> Give children a chance to practice.

> Pair children to practice together.

> Use a variety of illustrations, like pictures, videos, and drawings that show content.

> Ask questions and observe to be sure children understand.

> Provide positive encouragement and support as children try new skills.

Check in frequently. Don't assume children are "catching on." Check in frequently and give children multiple ways to show their understanding informally, as follows:

> Invite children to point to pictures or use illustrations to discuss story sequences and events.

> Play games and match items where children can show their knowledge.

> Encourage small and paired group activities for peer reinforcement.

> Provide many ways for children to represent and practice what they know by speaking, drawing, demonstrating, and writing or representing their ideas.

Make support personal. Each child has different background knowledge and understanding. The following questions will keep your approach individualized:

> When new concepts, content, or vocabulary are introduced, have you connected to each child's life experiences and language? How do you know? What is the child's response to the new information?

> How easily does this child engage with activities and peers? What additional supports will facilitate his or her comfort getting started and joining activities?

> How does this child understand and process information? Are there additional cues, props, examples, or language modeling that you could use to create a deeper context for understanding?

> Are you certain this child understands instructions and expectations? How do you know? What else can you do to be sure each child feels confident about directions and tasks?

> What special interests and abilities does this child have that you can encourage and support? What roles or tasks will strengthen this child's sense of belonging and connection to the classroom?

> How frequently does this child interact with different groups of children and participate in a variety of activities? What can you do to strengthen his or her peer relationships and extend participation in new and varied activities?

READY RESOURCES

Strategies for
Multilingual Learners

The following resources provide information and strategies for supporting multilingual learners through child-centered teaching:

> NAEYC provides resources to welcome and support dual language learners: NAEYC.org/resources/topics/dual-language-learners

> The World-Class Instructional Design and Assessment (WIDA) Standards and Can Do Descriptors provide language development resources for those who support the academic

success of multilingual learners. WIDA Early Years is a program focused specifically on the language development of young multilingual children in early care and education settings: https://wida.wisc.edu/taxonomy/term/81

> The WIDA *Early English Language Development Standards*: https://wida.wisc.edu/sites/default/files/resource/Early-ELD-Standards-Guide-2014-Edition.pdf

> The Total Physical Response approach shows how to use physical movement with verbal input when introducing new vocabulary: www.theteachertoolkit.com/index.php/tool/total-physical-response-tpr

> The Sheltered Instruction Observation Protocol model is a research-based instructional model with strategies to support English learners: www.cal.org/siop/resources

Using Individualized Support

Mr. Aaron finishes reading *The Snowy Day,* by Ezra Jack Keats, to Cassidy and Tessa during free play. He asks, "Why do you think Peter wanted to save his snowball?" Cassidy says, "He didn't want the snow to melt." Tessa adds, "He wanted to keep the snowball in his pocket." Mr. Aaron asks, "Why was Peter's pocket wet?" Cassidy looks sad. "It melted." "Yes indeed," agrees Mr. Aaron. "That frozen snowball turned into water. Peter felt sad because his pocket was empty and damp."

Mr. Aaron then asks, "Are you ready to play with snow or would you like to dress the snowman?" "I'm going to build a snow*girl*," says Cassidy. "I'm gonna make a snow angel," says Tessa. Mr. Aaron helps Tessa slip on gloves. "I want gloves too!" says Cassidy. As he helps Cassidy, Mr. Aaron asks, "After you pack the snow with your warm hands, what do you think will happen?" Cassidy replies, "It's going to melt." Tessa says, "It's going to get soggy." Mr. Aaron says, "Let's see what will happen."

Mr. Aaron introduces books about winter to challenge children's thinking about melting and freezing. Snow tubs are prepared with scoops and cups. Tessa doesn't like touching sand and water, so a supply of small, purple, powder- and latex-free gloves are ready. Tessa doesn't feel singled out, as Cassidy wears gloves too.

Across the room, children wrap a scarf around a cardboard snowman made from boxes. The children wear knitted mittens and hats as they pretend to play outside. This winter-themed dramatic play reflects their real-life experiences.

Chapter 1 explained that differentiation allows all children to reach learning goals by providing entry points, learning tasks, and outcomes tailored to children's learning needs. Mr. Aaron talks with children alone and in groups, varies the pacing, and explains information in multiple ways. He offers choices and provides a range of materials and challenge levels. He lets the girls show and tell him what they know in different ways.

When Mr. Aaron assists Tessa with gloves, this is an individualized learning strategy. *Individualization* relates to strategies, goals, methods, materials, and accommodations that support the success of specific children (Horn & Banerjee 2009). Individualization is both practical and personal. Individualized teaching can be seen in your space and setting, in material choices and arrangement, and in the level and type of support given. This is a proactive strategy that prepares for and responds to individual children's needs (Israel, Ribuffo, & Smith 2014).

During the pre-K year, all children can benefit from individualization. NAEYC's position statement "Developmentally Appropriate Practice" (2020) notes that this approach is part of universal design for learning, where all children receive the support they need to experience success. In this way, individualization is not limited to the goals established in a child's individualized education program (IEP).

In your lesson plan, you can include a section for individualization that names specific children and details strategies designed just for them (see Chapter 4). You can use space to write notes about what worked well and modify or update strategies.

In a classic resource by Linda Crane Mitchell (2004), the author states that children develop skills more easily when they are embedded in authentic play activities. She provides an acronym, MOST, which offers guidance on making changes to materials, objectives, space, and time.

> **Materials:** Modify the ease of material use (e.g., tape paper to table, provide larger brushes), add special items, vary tactile or visual stimulation, and provide modeling and verbal support.

> **Objectives:** Select learning or IEP goals and support these during play.

> **Space:** Plan for adaptive equipment (e.g., wheelchairs) and ensure ample or modified spaces that work best for each child.

> **Time:** Allow for additional or flexible time to complete activities and adjust the number of activities to match children's ability to manage them.

To individualize effectively, you'll need to ask families to explain what works well at home. You can incorporate these ideas into your teaching approaches. Shared analysis ensures that you understand children's development and adjust your approaches as needed.

TIPS FOR TEACHING
Supporting Children with Special Needs

When making adaptations for children with disabilities, you'll need to first have a solid understanding of each child's independent and emerging skills as well as identify specific areas that need support. Next, you'll evaluate the activity. What skills will children need to use to be successful in manipulating materials, using spaces, understanding goals, and interacting with others? These skills include

> **Auditory needs.** What will children need to hear and process?

> **Communication needs.** What will children need to understand, document, and express? Will they use language to plan, organize, and ask questions? Is assistive technology needed to promote full access and participation?

> **Visual needs.** What will children need to see, distinguish, or organize visually?

> **Fine motor activity.** What materials will children need to touch and manipulate?

> **Gross motor activity.** What movement is required of the body? Is there freedom to get up, move around, and access physical spaces and materials?

> **Kinesthetic and tactile sensitivity.** Do children have sensitivities to certain textures and materials? Do they have fears or restrictions about touching or engaging with materials?

> **Stimulation.** Is there adequate stimulation so children have the appropriate level of challenge? Is there distraction from light, noise, or close proximity to other children? Can children access both active and quiet spaces and experiences?

> **Executive function (e.g., attention, memory, planning, self-direction).** Is there adequate preparation for upcoming tasks or events? What specific executive function skills will children need to be successful?

> **Social competence (e.g., managing emotions, expressing emotions, recognizing emotions).** What supports are needed to prepare, monitor, and execute tasks? What social supports will be needed for sharing materials, problem solving, handling frustrations, and feeling confident?

> **Learning needs.** Is there a rich context for children to make sense of information? For example, do teachers use stories, visual aids, pictures, videos, role-play, and hands-on materials? Are new ideas connected to children's cultures, languages, families, and personal lives? Are multistep procedures demonstrated and scaffolded?

Successful inclusion involves communication and collaboration with children and families. It involves reflective participation among all staff who interact with children. When you talk together, you'll want to review all aspects of the classroom—the setting, materials, supports, and activities—that influence the way children respond. You will continue to adapt spaces, materials, tools, and supports to create the best possible circumstances for each child's success.

READY RESOURCES

Key Components of Inclusive Programs

> NAEYC and the Division for Early Childhood's joint position statement "Early Childhood Inclusion" provides a blueprint for identifying the key components of high-quality inclusive programs and recommendations for how the position statement should be used by families, practitioners, administrators, policy makers, and others to improve early childhood services: NAEYC.org/sites/default/files/globally-shared/downloads/PDFs/resources/position-statements/DEC_NAEYC_EC_updatedKS.pdf

> The US Department of Education's Individuals with Disabilities Education Act website provides information and resources about children with disabilities: https://sites.ed.gov/idea/?src=ft

> The Centers for Disease Control and Prevention provides links to other websites with resources about developmental disabilities: www.cdc.gov/ncbddd/developmentaldisabilities/links.html

Sample Lesson Plans

Connecting Learning Across Content Areas

When designing lesson plans for play activities, consider the following questions:

> **Early learning standards:** What developmental skills and academic concepts will you teach?

> **Learning objectives:** What will children be learning and practicing during an activity?

> **Concepts and big ideas:** What higher-level concepts or big ideas are children discovering?

> **Vocabulary:** What vocabulary would you like children to understand and use?

> **Connections to children's life context:** What explicit connections to children's experiences, families, communities, languages, and cultures are present?

> **Reflection:** What did you notice about this play activity? What did work well and why? What did not work well and why?

As you begin child-centered lesson planning, an important goal is to layer children's experiences so they have multiple opportunities to explore concepts and ideas—and many ways to reinforce their understanding. The lesson plan in Figure 3.1 will help you integrate content learning across play areas.

Sample Lesson Plan

Theme: Families

Big Ideas and Concepts	Questions and Prompts

Big Ideas and Concepts

> Children develop identity and belonging with families.

> Family culture includes language, places, foods, people, activities, music, poetry, and conversations.

> Shared culture makes families special.

> Families are alike and different.

> Families visit families, friends, and places together.

> Families care for and help each other.

> Photos, drawings, and music tell personal stories just like written stories and reflect the cultural background and beauty of children and their families.

Content Vocabulary: names for family members; *adventure, celebrations/traditions, destination, ingredient, journey/travel, market/store, real/ pretend, relative/related, respect* and *fairness, unique/different, work/occupation*

Academic Vocabulary: *compare, decide, sequence, sort*

Questions and Prompts

> How do you help your family? How does your family help you?

> How are families the same? How are they different?

> What places do you visit? What is your favorite destination?

> What special events (activities, songs, books) do you enjoy with your family?

> What meals do you cook with your family?

> How do you know if something happened in the past or present?

> What manners do you use at home and school? How do you show respect?

Activities and Materials for Play and Learning Areas

Reading/Library Area	Writing Area	Mathematics Area
Standards	**Standards**	**Standards**
RI.PK.10: Actively participate in read aloud experiences using age appropriate information books individually and in small and large groups.	W.PK.2: Use a combination of drawings, dictation, scribble writing, letter-strings, or invented spelling to share information during play or other activities.	4.1: Children begin to demonstrate an understanding of number and counting. 4.3: Children begin to conceptualize measurable attributes of objects and how to measure them.
Family Books 〉 *Abuela,* by Arthur Dorros 〉 *City Shapes,* by Diana Murray 〉 *Dream Dancer,* by Jill Newsome 〉 *Grandma's Gift* and *Grandma's Records,* by Eric Velasquez 〉 *I Love Saturdays y domingos,* by Alma Flor Ada 〉 *In My Family/En mi familia,* by Carmen Lomas Garza 〉 *Kamik, an Inuit Puppy* (series), by Matilda Sulurayok 〉 *Last Stop on Market Street,* by Matt de la Peña 〉 *Marisol McDonald Doesn't Match,* by Monica Brown 〉 *My Name is Yoon,* by Helen Recorvits 〉 *Where Are You From?* by Yamile Saied Méndez 〉 *Whoever You Are,* by Mem Fox	**Materials** 〉 Note cards, pens, pencils, stamps, and mailbox (box with slit) to write or dictate thank-you letters to families 〉 Class notebook with page for each child to draw pictures and write or dictate a family story. "My family went to the . . ." 〉 Letter stamps and ink pads for child and family names	**Materials** 〉 People and accessories to sort by attributes (shorter and taller, more and less) 〉 Paper and pencils or board and markers for graphing numbers of siblings and pets 〉 Family Fun board game (counting cubes, file-folder board): Pass community sites (e.g., zoo, school, fire station, store) to reach the park with your family 〉 Rulers and measuring tapes for body math (measuring how tall you are and the length of your feet and arms)

continues

Fine Motor Area	Science and Nature Area	Music and Movement Area
Standards	**Standards**	**Standards**
9.1.2: Show curiosity and initiative by choosing to explore a variety of activities and experiences with a willingness to try new challenges (e.g., choosing harder and harder puzzles).	5.1.5: Represent observations and work through drawing, recording data, and "writing" (e.g., drawing and "writing" on observation clipboards, making rubbings, charting the growth of plants).	1.1.5: Participate in or observe a variety of dance and movement activities accompanied by music and/or props from different cultures and genres. 9.2.3: Use multiple means of communication to creatively express thoughts, ideas, and feelings (e.g., sing a song and act out the story of the life cycle of a butterfly).

Fine Motor Area

Materials

> Memory game (laminated photos of children)

> Family Go Fish cards

> Jigsaw puzzles created from family photos

> Day in the Life (card sort showing daily family activities)

> Past to Present (sorting or sequencing photos from baby to present)

> Various manipulatives to build family homes

Science and Nature Area

Materials

> Leaf, plant, bark, and branch collections from backyards and magnifying glasses

> Paper, pencils, and crayons for natural collection drawing and rubbing to compare size, shape, and other attributes

> Metal objects from home for magnet play

Music and Movement Area

Materials

Listening Library

> "Hello, Neighbor" (Dr. Jean)

> "Finger Family Song" (Brain Boogie Boosters, The Learning Station)

> "Katie Is Important" (Dr. Jean)

> "The More We Get Together" (Traditional)

> "We Are a Family" (Jack Hartmann)

Movement

> Dance costumes, scarves, and a child-safe, full-length mirror

> Music representing the home cultures of children (e.g., Putumayo, World Playground)

Instruments

> To typical instrument collection, add hand drums, tambourines, maracas, rhythm sticks, conga, and djembe (or homemade drums from containers) to prompt chants or raps about families

continues

Dramatic Play Area	Block Area	Art Area
Standards	**Standards**	**Standards**
9.2.1: Show flexibility in approaching tasks by being open to new ideas (i.e., doesn't cling to one approach to a task, but is willing to experiment and to risk trying out a new idea or approach).	9.1.3: Focus attention on tasks and experiences, despite interruptions or distractions (e.g., working hard on a drawing even when children nearby are playing a game).	1.4: Children express themselves through and develop an appreciation of the visual arts (e.g., painting, sculpting, and drawing).
Materials and Prop Boxes	**Materials**	**Materials**
❯ *People we visit*: suitcases, backpacks, clothing ❯ *Family cooking/setting the table*: kitchen utensils (e.g., whisk, potato masher, sifter, pastry blender, rolling pin, tongs, apple corer), recipe book, apron, chef hat, mixing bowls, wok, tea set ❯ *Helping our families:* brooms, dusters, laundry, watering plants, putting clothes away, shopping ❯ *Family pets:* stuffed animals with pet care items ❯ *How families go to sleep:* blankets, pillows, dolls, diapers, baby bottles, sound machine ❯ Practicing manners we use at home/introducing family members	❯ People and small house accessories with challenge to build home or street ❯ Book: *City Shapes*, by Diana Murray ❯ Hollow blocks made from grocery boxes from children's homes (e.g., rice, cereal, tissues, sugar) ❯ Building from drawn sketches of children's homes, apartments, buildings, or living spaces	❯ Collage using magazine pictures of families ❯ Easels, paint, and paintbrushes to create house paintings to hang on classroom family tree ❯ Hand and thumbprint art ❯ Puppet of "me" with cardboard tubes, fabric, rubber bands, and markers or paint ❯ Drawing my face with a mirror ❯ Children's body outline to be colored and decorated

Figure 3.1. Sample lesson plan demonstrating how to integrate content learning across play areas. (Standards from New Jersey State Department of Education [2014].)

Sample Book Lists

Aiming for Big Ideas and Concepts

As you begin to build out lesson plans, you'll find that books can serve as an inspiration. Begin with a book list and materials for dramatic play. As you identify the big ideas and concepts, you'll see how to fit your state or curriculum early learning guidelines with the reality of gathering materials and choosing materials and activities.

Animals

> *A Is for Animals,* by Tom Lemler

> *Carl* (series), by Alexandra Day

> *Forest Life and Woodland Creatures,* by DK

> *My Pet Wants a Pet,* by Elise Broach and Eric Barclay

> *National Geographic Little Kids First Big Books* (series), by Catherine Hughes

> *Please, Puppy, Please,* by Spike Lee and Tonya Lewis Lee

> *Strictly No Elephants,* by Lisa Mantchev

> Various animal books by Cari Meister

> Various animal books by Jan Brett

> *Where Animals Live* (series), by John Wood

Health and Nutrition

> *Bread, Bread, Bread,* by Ann Morris

> *Eating the Alphabet,* by Lois Ehlert

> *Food Parade: Healthy Eating with the Nutritious Food Groups,* by Elicia Castaldi

> *From Seed to Plant,* by Gail Gibbons

> *Good Enough to Eat: A Kid's Guide to Food and Nutrition,* by Lizzy Rockwell

> *My Food, Your Food,* by Lisa Bullard

> *Oranges to Orange Juice,* by Inez Snyder

> *Something Good,* by Robert Munsch

> *The Vegetables We Eat,* by Gail Gibbons

> *What's in the Garden?* by Marianne Berkes

Housekeeping and Cooking

> *Community Soup,* by Alma Fullerton

> *Cora Cooks Pancit,* by Dorina K. Lazo Gilmore

> *Feast for 10,* by Cathryn Falwell

> *Green Is a Chile Pepper: A Book of Colors,* by Roseanne Greenfield Thong

> *It's Pancake Time,* by A.D. Largie

> *Mama Panya's Pancakes: A Village Tale from Kenya,* by Mary and Rich Chamberlin

> *Round Is a Tortilla: A Book of Shapes,* by Roseanne Greenfield Thong

> *Stone Soup,* by Jon J. Muth

> *Thank You, Omu!* by Oge Mora

> *What Should I Make?* by Nandini Nayer

Recycling and Nature

> *The Adventures of a Plastic Bottle: A Story About Recycling*, by Alison Inches

> *The Adventures of an Aluminum Can: A Story About Recycling*, by Alison Inches

> *The Berenstain Bears Go Green*, by Jan and Mike Berenstain

> *Compost Stew: An A to Z Recipe for the Earth*, by Mary McKenna Siddals

> *Curious George: Trash into Treasure*, by H.A. Rey

> *Down the Drain: Conserving Water*, by Anita Ganeri

> *I Can Save the Earth! One Little Monster Learns to Reduce, Reuse, and Recycle*, by Alison Inches

> *Recycle! A Handbook for Kids*, by Gail Gibbons

> *Recycle Every Day!* by Nancy Elizabeth Wallace

> *We Planted a Tree*, by Diane Muldrow

Social-Emotional Learning

> *Do Unto Otters: A Book About Manners*, by Laurie Keller

> *Finding Kindness*, by Deborah Underwood

> *Full, Full, Full of Love*, by Trish Cooke

> *Have You Filled a Bucket Today? A Guide to Daily Happiness for Kids*, by Carol McCloud

> *Hey Jasmine! Let's Go to the Park*, by Amber Nichole and Mike Motz

> *It's Not Working, Daddy: Kids Learn to Do It for Themselves*, by A.D. Largie

> *Kindness Starts with You, At School*, by Jacquelyn Stagg

> *The Emperor's Egg*, by Martin Jenkins and Jane Chapman

> *The Way I Feel*, by Janan Cain

> *Today I Feel Silly: And Other Moods That Make My Day*, by Jamie Lee Curtis

Weather

> *Clouds*, by Anne Rockwell

> *The Mitten*, by Jan Brett

> *National Geographic Little Kids First Big Book of Weather*, by Karne de Seve

> *Oh Say Can You Say What's the Weather Today? All About Weather*, by Tish Rabe

> *Sunshine Makes the Seasons*, by Franklyn M. Branley

> *The Snowy Day*, by Ezra Jack Keats

> *The Umbrella*, by Jan Brett

> *Weather Words and What They Mean*, by Gail Gibbons

> *What Will the Weather Be?* by Lynda DeWitt

> *Wow! Weather!* by Paul Deanno

To create a high-quality classroom, you'll need to nurture positive social interactions as well as rich learning experiences. The NAEYC Early Learning Program Accreditation Standards and Assessment Items support the lesson planning approaches of this chapter. Topic 1.D presents classroom environments in which limits are clear, bias is countered, and pro-social behavior is promoted. Topic 4.D addresses adapting curriculum, individualized teaching, and informing program development.

Development and learning goals are given with strategies for practice. These include

> 1.F—Promoting Self-Regulation

> 2.A—Essential Characteristics

> 2.B—Social and Emotional Development

> 2.C—Physical Development

> 2.D—Language Development

> 2.E—Early Literacy

> 2.F—Early Mathematics

> 2.G—Science

> 2.H—Technology

> 2.J—Creative Expression and Appreciation for the Arts

> 2.K—Health and Safety

> 2.L—Social Studies

Standard 3—Teaching provides guidance for daily planning and interactions, including

> 3.A—Designing Enriched Learning Environments

> 3.B—Creating Caring Communities for Learning

> 3.C—Supervising Children

> 3.D—Using Time, Grouping, and Routines to Achieve Learning Goals

> 3.E—Responding to Children's Interests and Needs

> 3.F—Making Learning Meaningful for All Children

> 3.G—Using Instruction to Deepen Children's Understanding and Build Their Skills and Knowledge

REFLECTION QUESTIONS

1. Which play areas in your classroom currently work well to support learning? What engages children and why?

2. After reviewing this chapter, the sample lesson plan, and the sample book lists, what do you notice about your current lesson plans that you would like to change or improve?

3. How would you like to change or improve your materials, spaces, and interactions to more effectively engage children in language, literacy, social-emotional, and content area learning?

4. As you plan a new play activity, what steps can you take to adjust, adapt, or modify materials, objectives, space, and time to better engage and support learning for children with special needs?

CHAPTER 4

Planning Teacher-Directed Activities

Introducing New Information

Ms. Celia places a tub of cold water in front of her. She pours a bowl of ice cubes and places a disc-shaped piece of ice in the water, where it floats. Then she places a plastic penguin on top of the ice island. "How do you think Penguin will stay warm when he swims in the water?" She invites the children to touch the water with a finger. "Ohh! It's cold." They giggle. "His feathers will keep him warm," says Evea. "He'll close his eyes under water," suggests Isan. "Maybe his body will keep him warm," says Nylahni. "Yes. All those will help keep him warm—the feathers, the body fat, and keeping his eyes closed!"

"When you take a bath, is your bath water cold?" Ms. Celia asks the children. The children laugh. "No! We would freeze," says Amie dramatically. "I like my water hot," says Zachary. "I like mine with bubbles," says Siena. "So," Ms. Celia continues, "why can't you stay warm in the cold water, but penguins can stay warm?" "Oh that's easy," says Javion. "I don't have feathers. I just got hair on my head." Ms. Celia responds, "That's right. People have smooth skin with no protection. But the penguins have soft feathers next to their skin. The feathers are very short and fluffy and waterproof. The water cannot get inside. Even the ice slides right off. The feathers keep penguin bodies warm and dry."

Ms. Celia places a small white feather in each of the children's hands. "Can you feel how soft it is? Do you see the tiny spikes? Those are called *vanes*. The air blows over the surface of the feather, and water rolls off—like a raincoat." The children are very still as they rub their fingers up and down the feathers. Ms. Celia adds, "To stay warm, you need to wear a winter coat or a raincoat, but penguins already have feathers. Your raincoat provides protection and acts as a barrier to the water. A barrier means water and cold cannot touch the penguin's skin."

When Ms. Celia plans her group lesson, she decides to demonstrate ice water with a plastic penguin to help the children imagine how the animal can stay warm. She uses the ice water as a way to make the life of a penguin real to the children. In her lesson plan, she calls this feature an *anticipatory set*. Some programs refer to this activity as the introduction or motivator.

This active, hands-on activity engages children's senses and helps them compare their comfort in a warm bath to a penguin's sensations in icy water. The white feathers, borrowed from art supplies, help the children understand body coverings.

The purpose of an anticipatory set or introduction is to present new ideas and concepts. While you may ask children to remember a previous lesson or ask what they already know, the main goal is to help children understand new concepts and vocabulary. During this introduction, Ms. Celia uses the words *vane*, *protection*, and *barrier*. She will reinforce these ideas as she visits and talks with the children in play areas.

TIPS FOR TEACHING

Connecting to Children's Daily Lives

When introducing new information, be certain it makes sense to each child. Not all children have the same background knowledge, so it's important to have materials available to introduce new concepts or topics. Consider the following questions:

> What activity and accompanying materials can you use to show (rather than talk about) a concept?

> What book, poster, or photo will illustrate details about this concept?

> What similar experiences do children understand that relate to this concept?

> How does the new information add to what children already know?

> How can you help children understand the topic in a more complex way? For example, what are contributing factors? What else can help children learn more?

> How does this activity help children understand each other? Do all people or animals feel the same way? Are there other perspectives?

> How can you encourage children to share their ideas and experiences?

> How does this activity add to children's value and appreciation of the topic?

> How can children represent their learning in a way that makes sense to them? Can they draw or paint the concept, reenact a situation during play, or retell a story?

Engaging Children in Higher-Level Thinking

Ms. Celia holds up the book *20 Facts About Penguins*, by Heather Moore Niver. "Yesterday, we identified parts of the penguin's body. What do you remember?" The children answer, "Body, face, eyes, mouth, beak, and feathers."

Ms. Celia prompts, "Do you remember what's on the side of the penguin's body?" The children shout, "Flippers!" "That's right," Ms. Celia smiles. "Penguins use flippers to keep them steady when they waddle on the ice." The children laugh loudly and say, "Waddle!" She goes on, "They use flippers to keep them steady when they slide on their tummies and land in the water. When a group of penguins is all together on land, we call them a *waddle*. But when they are all together in the water, we call them a *raft*. Why do you think they are called a waddle and a raft?" Jasper says, "They waddle on the land." Abdul says, "They float like a raft."

"What's that?" asks Jasper. He points to the picture in the book. Ms. Celia says, "That is an emperor penguin. An emperor is like a king." "He looks like a king," says Javion. "What's that one?" Ms. Celia points again. This is a crested penguin with head feathers. Can you see the feather hat? And there is a macaroni penguin." The children respond, "Macaroni!" "And this is a rock penguin!" The children respond, "Rock!"

Ms. Celia says, "Penguins come in many sizes and kinds—just like we do. They waddle side by side to keep warm. They use mud and plants to build their nests." As she finishes the book, Ms. Celia says, "Let's make a chart to document the activities of penguins."

Ms. Celia draws a graphic organizer circle on a large paper clipped to the interactive writing board. She tapes a photo of a penguin to the inside of the circle. On the outside spokes, she writes what the children tell her penguins do. They swim in cold water; slide on the ice; eat squid, krill, and fish; feed their babies; build nests; live in a colony; and live in Antarctica. Her goal is to move beyond rote answers and help the children think in more complex ways about the lives of animals.

Ms. Celia clips the paper to the board. She tells the children they will discover more about penguins during center play. In the reading area basket, she includes a copy of the *20 Fun Facts* book along with *Penguins, Penguins, Everywhere!* by Bob Barner; *Penguins,* by Cherie Winner (Our Wild World); and *Penguins*, by Ann Wendorff (Oceans Alive). She gives the children a stuffed penguin, donated by a family, that the children can cuddle while they read.

This book reading and conversation—while responsive to children's questions and ideas—was carefully planned. Ms. Celia reviewed several books before choosing this one. She made a list of vocabulary words, including *squid, krill, colony, beak, flippers, waddle,* and *raft.* She printed pictures of each animal to hold up and show the children as she read. She wrote the questions on a card and used it to lead the conversation. She reviewed the thematic books for the reading area and prepared play areas for more exposure to learning.

Because the book reading sparks the children's curiosity about penguins, they are highly engaged. They respond eagerly to the graphic organizer activity. When Ms. Celia asks which children want to read more, all hands shoot up. They are eager to look more closely at the pictures of the penguins with the funny names. Ms. Celia enjoys seeing the children's excitement as they talk about the animals.

Rather than focus on rote or memorized skills, your teaching can foster critical thinking skills (Wellberg 2019). These include identifying similarities and differences, sorting objects by attribute (classifying), defining and explaining concepts, and asking meaningful questions to learn more. Questions should promote reasoning, such as "How do you know?" "How can you tell?" or "Why do you think that happened?" Children can apply the process of critical thinking and asking questions to other learning situations.

TIPS FOR TEACHING

Choosing a Method and Activity

In teacher-directed learning, while the teacher takes the lead, activities are child-centered and children have many choices. What format works best to introduce a new idea or skill? Consider the following questions as you plan:

> How will you introduce the idea? What will you say and do?

> What questions will you ask? How will you expect children to respond?

> What will you say to connect to children's experiences?

> If you read a book, what content is important?

> Will you model a skill? How will you teach this skill to children?

> How will you differentiate the lesson for different skill levels, including language skill?

> What real objects, demonstrations, and conversations will you have that involve children's participation?

> How will you use guided and independent practice?

> Will you include a summary or review of what was learned?

> What additional resources will children need to integrate new vocabulary and ideas into conversations and play?

Following a Sequence of Planning

During dramatic play, Ms. Celia shows Chu how to buckle the closure on his backpack. It is stuffed with travel clothing. She says, "I'm the customs inspector and you have to show me your passport." Chu opens his passport book, and Ms. Celia gives him a stamp. He says, "Put it on the Antarctica page."

Ms. Celia comments, "I wonder what clothes will keep you warm." Chu responds, "I packed my sweater and my Oreos. I don't want to be hungry." She adds, "You'd better bring some long underwear, too. You don't have down feathers like penguin."

Ms. Celia continues, "Do you have your science journal? You'll need it to study the animals." Chu follows Ms. Celia's lead and tucks in a journal. She offers the basket of knitted accessories. Chu pulls out red mittens and a blue cap.

Ms. Celia engages with children after book reading. She's interested in modeling play for children in the dramatic play area. Then she visits the ice-water tub to help children put on gloves. She asks them which gloves they predict will keep them warmest. Across the room, Ms. Karla assists the children by writing their dictated stories and helping them spell words. Both teachers are delighted to see the children's enthusiasm and engagement.

The following sequence will help you follow along with Ms. Celia's lesson plans for the penguin activity with extensions for each of the play areas. The standards she uses are from the Illinois State Pre-K Language Arts Standards (ISBE 2020). The lesson plan elements included the following:

1. **List of standards.** 3.B.ECa: Identify basic similarities and differences in pictures and information. 2.B.ECa: Ask and answer questions about book read aloud. 5.B.ECa: Use a combination of drawing, dictating, or writing to express ideas about a topic. 12.A.ECa: Observe, investigate, describe, and categorize living things.

2. **Learning goals (big ideas, concept learning).** Children will understand penguin attributes and habitats, concepts of living together in groups (colony), protection and adaptation to habitats, and activities of penguins.

3. **Content and academic vocabulary.** Content words: *insulation*, *prey*, *predator*, *protection*, *waddle*, and *slide*. Academic words: *compare*, *chart*, and *predict*.

4. **Introduction/anticipatory set.** Ice-water tub activity to contrast with children's current knowledge about warm-water baths. Feather introduction to connect with children's understanding about jackets and coats that provide protection.

5. **Teaching activity.** First, show photos of penguins and label body parts. Second, read *20 Facts About Penguins*. Ask children to describe (1) parts of a penguin, (2) differences children see between penguins' bodies and their own bodies, (3) how penguins use their bodies, and (4) activities of penguins. Finally, engage children in documentation of penguin activities using a graphic organizer.

6. **Extended learning concepts into play area activities.** Integrated learning includes "building out" teacher-directed activities into child-directed play activities and responses. When children experience multiple exposures to new information, they dig deeper and learn more. They have time to develop higher-level understanding and explore more complex ideas. When developing more extended lesson plans, notice how children

interact with materials and identify what best engages their interest. Play areas will become impactful, vital spaces that increase children's learning and discovery. For example

> During dramatic play, the children plan a trip to Antarctica. They pack food and clothes and pretend to ride in a boat. They bring binoculars made from cardboard tubes, passports that they use with stamp pads, and maps.

> In the reading area, children explore a range of books about animals in the Arctic and Antarctic. They enjoy holding the two small cloth penguins.

> In the math area, children play number matching games and a board game, moving their penguin pieces from iceberg to iceberg. The games are teacher-drawn on file folders.

> In the science area are bowls of feathers, fur samples, and a fish model. Children talk about why animals need different kinds of skin coverings. They look at scales, fur, and feathers and draw these in science journals. The question prompt is "What do animals wear?" The children look at *Feathers and Hair: What Animals Wear*, by Jennifer Ward, through magnifying glasses. Laminated photos from the Smithsonian's National Zoo and Conservation Biology Institute (https://nationalzoo. si.edu/animals) are stacked in a basket.

> In the technology area, the children keep an eye on the penguin camera at the San Diego Zoo (https://zoo. sandiegozoo.org/cams/penguin-cam).

> In the writing area, children dictate a story about a penguin family. They brainstorm words that start with the letters in the word *penguin*. Postcards are ready for notes the children send home to their families from their Antarctica exploration trip.

> In the art center, children tear tissue paper to create a penguin colony collage and to show penguins playing. Animal photos are provided on the table to inspire creative ideas.

> At the water table, ice cubes are added. Children compare the warmth of a down glove, plastic gloves, and a double baggy filled with Crisco to see which keeps their hands warmest.

> In block play, children are challenged to build caves and penguin nests. Plastic penguins and flat pebbles have been added as an accessory. Here, the children look at the illustrations in *If You Were a Penguin,* by Wendell and Florence Minor, and *Penguins,* by Maria De Lorena.

> In the fine motor area, penguin puzzles are created from photos secured to cardboard and cut into pieces. The penguin parts are labeled. The three-part puzzles are fun for the children, with the head, middle, and feet pieces ready to mix and match.

These play areas are designed to build on the teacher-directed lessons for a two-week period. Materials are added and changed, so that children encounter books, puzzles, art materials, play props, and other activities to keep pace with new ideas and concepts. As the theme shifts, new materials and activities are rotated in and out.

7. **Observing and documenting children's learning.** During free play, the teachers talk frequently with children about their play. They use a checklist to document each child's use of new vocabulary, their ability to identify penguin body parts, and their understanding of how body coverings help animals stay warm. In addition to the checklist, they write notes about what children say and enjoy.

What is the best way to evaluate and document children's progress? Will children draw pictures or construct something? Will writing their dictation motivate their storytelling? Will photographs or a video best capture their work and play? What kinds of documentation should go in their learning portfolios? Explore Chapter 6 for answers to these questions. Chapter 5 provides other ways to document children's learning in authentic ways using photos, videos, and samples of children's work.

A practical lesson plan describes what to say, how to make connections to children's lives, and questions to guide conversations. It helps to identify needed vocabulary and skills and plan activities and materials that engage children's exploration of specific content. Mapping out these details will result in a higher level of engagement for the children and will lead to longer times of absorbed play.

TIPS FOR TEACHING

Infusing the Joy of Writing

Have you noticed the joy children demonstrate as they begin to use writing to document and share ideas? Young children discover practical ways to use writing as they make lists, begin to write stories, and share their ideas. In the world of quick sound bites and all forms of digital writing, written expression is still a critical skill for college and career. Here are some ideas to demonstrate the useful purposes of writing and to inspire engagement:

> Ask children to add ideas to a "What do we want to know?" list. Model the writing and help children add to the list.

> Use dictation so children can watch you writing their words. It's very exciting for them to hear their ideas read back to them.

> Invite children to write postcards or letters with pictures and share them with families.

> Add writing tools and papers to play areas. Include graph paper with a pencil and clipboard to the block area for designing structures. Add shopping lists, calendars, doctor pads, police tickets, menus, and sales receipt books to the housekeeping area. Add a science journal for children to capture drawings and ideas in the science area.

> Design an appealing writing center by adding paper with a variety of colors, textures, and sizes. Include multiple writing tools of multiple sizes and shapes, including pens, pencils (e.g., wood, colored), markers, and crayons. Add envelopes, "stamps," and a "mailbox." Include thicker paper for sign making with wider-tipped markers.

> At the writing center, include tape, staplers, and other interesting clips for children to attach papers when they create books, design pockets, or create other writing items.

> Organize the writing area with items stored in baskets and containers for easy viewing and access.

> Place the alphabet and "favorite words" on or near the writing table.

> Ask children to create a word wall with pictures using four-by-six-inch cards.

> Model how to write group poems and silly stories. Introduce a sentence prompt and ask the children to add on with their ideas and words. Model writing for the children using a large anchor chart. When they are able to add words, include them in the writing process.

> Invite children to be active participants in labeling their drawings, artwork, and other work.

> Ask community workers and families to write a letter to your class. For example, ask the police chief, a firefighter, a doctor, a musician, or the librarian to write and include interesting events or details about their work. The letters can be brief, and receiving mail is thrilling for young children.

> Children enjoy clipping their writing and drawings to a clothesline. Add a "letter line" above the writing table or in a special area located nearby.

> Label areas of the classroom and items in the children's home languages. Rather than do this independently, invite the children and families to be part of the process over time. The participation and modeling are important so that children notice and understand the word labels.

Focus on practical uses for writing and the joy of expressing oneself with words. Encourage children to write a poem about science or math. Ask them to put notes into a box to describe things they love and enjoy. Call it *Favorite Things,* and support children's ideas by asking them to draw what they are thinking about. You can take dictation or support their early writing. Select several notes to read each morning. Weave these ideas into your lesson plans, and children will be thrilled to recognize their contributions.

Field Note: Keeping Displays Current

When my classroom play areas are aligned with a theme, it's easier to keep classroom displays current. Children are proud to see their stories, photos, and artwork hung where they can see and talk about them. I ask them to clip their own paintings on the art line. I offer a tape dispenser so they can put their drawings and other work on the wall. We have an art museum on a shelf, and they write labels for three-dimensional projects and dried dough pieces. At the end of each week, I send items home for families. Then we start over! While some displays stay longer, I try to cycle what is on the walls to match our current unit of learning.

RESEARCH CONNECTIONS

Creating a Rich Contact Zone for Learning

Research shows that even when different teachers use the same curriculum, children's experiences differ vastly (Jenkins et al. 2019). Children can "expect a stunning level of variation from year to year and setting to setting in classroom experiences" (Pianta, Downer, & Hamre 2016, 130). Children need consistent exposure to pre-academic content, language-rich interactions, social-emotional scaffolding, and learning opportunities that are individualized throughout the day, including during play, meals, and routines (Pianta et al. 2018).

An important goal of the pre-K year is to prepare children academically and socially for kindergarten (Dotterer et al. 2013). Children need exposure to content with sufficient frequency, quality, and challenge to make learning gains (Beecher et al. 2017; Darrow 2013; McGuire et al. 2016). Even when curriculum is aligned with pre-K standards, children's learning depends on the effectiveness of instructional practices (Graue et al. 2018).

Children learn math, science, and literacy skills through specific modeling and teaching strategies (Gropen et al. 2017; Jenkins et al. 2018). Lesson planning focuses on the "what to teach" as well as the "how to teach," and ensures effective use of your specific setting and materials. But you also need to know the "why of teaching."

Why does teaching matter? High-quality instructional and social-emotional support, especially when sustained over time, predict greater language, literacy, and math skills (Carr et al. 2019). What does *high quality* look like? High-quality classrooms create a rich contact zone for children to engage with peers and adults in meaningful learning throughout each day.

Teaching Children with Special Needs

Mr. Jason reads *Grandfather Tang's Story*, by Ann Tompert. He stops reading to move the shapes on the magnetic board into the form of a fox and then into a rabbit. As he tells about the dog chasing a squirrel, the children's eyes get bigger. He reads, "Wu Ling transformed herself into a . . ." "Squirrel!" the children shout together. Mr. Jason continues with the story of the hawk, "And as he dove, he tucked in his beak and tail and legs, turned green, and changed into a . . ." "Turtle!" the children call out the missing word (Tompert 1997, 10).

Mr. Jason reads *Grandfather Tang's Story* to inspire the children to look for and describe shapes. In response to the story, he models how to use tangram pieces to create patterns that look like the fox, rabbit, dog, squirrel, hawk, and turtle. As he places the pieces together, he asks children to explain the attributes of each shape. After the story, the children will create new animal shapes with tangram pieces. They will draw animals using shape patterns they choose.

Mr. Jason understands that Charlie needs to have an unobstructed view during book reading. Mr. Jason wears a microphone that is clipped to his shirt because Charlie wears assistive hearing technology. Noriah chooses a stuffed animal to hold to help her focus. Victoria uses an individual copy of the book so that she can see the illustrations. These adaptations ensure the children can participate successfully.

Mr. Jason knows that George and Maddy will need to sit on opposite ends of the table from each other during the shape activity. This will minimize their frustration and allow them to concentrate. He knows that Grady and Nala must be able to pick up and manipulate the shape pieces. He includes tangrams with larger pieces and patterns. He attaches loops onto the pieces to make them easier to pick up. The children appreciate the rubber mat so their patterns do not slip. The practical adjustments minimize frustrations.

Mr. Jason evaluates the lesson plan for auditory and visual needs. He thinks about how children will listen, talk, and answer questions. He gives them options like thumbs-up responses and the opportunity to turn and talk with a peer partner to share answers and ideas. The school follows federal guidelines to ensure accessibility of doorways, bathrooms, and entryways. Mr. Jason ensures children can get around and use the indoor and outdoor spaces easily.

When planning activities, Mr. Jason makes sure children have many choices as they practice the skills he introduces. He monitors the light and noise level and watches out for situations where children are in close proximity to others. He wants to be sure children can participate fully and feel confident in their learning.

Meeting the needs of children means looking for practical and useful ways to ensure successful engagement with learning activities. NAEYC and other organizations provide many resources for working with children with disabilities:

> The *Teaching Young Children* article "Every Child Belongs: Welcoming a Child with a Disability," by Pamela Brillante, provides definitions and supports you can use: NAEYC.org/resources/pubs/tyc/sep2017/every-child-belongs

- NAEYC's Special Education topic webpage offers many articles and resources to help you be effective creating an inclusive classroom that meets the needs of diverse learners: NAEYC. org/resources/topics/special-education

- The Council for Exceptional Children (CEC) offers professional principles and standards for teaching, along with information about terms and definitions for exceptionalities and the latest news in special and gifted education: https://exceptionalchildren.org/ improving-your-practice/tools-and-resources

- The Division for Early Childhood of the Council for Exceptional Children (DEC) promotes policies and practices that support families and teachers in enhancing the optimal development of young children who have or are at risk for developmental delays and disabilities: www.dec-sped.org

- The Early Childhood Technical Assistance (ECTA) Center provides information about the appropriate use of assistive technology and provides resources to ensure the successful inclusion of young children with disabilities in early learning classrooms: www. ectacenter.org/topics/atech/atech.asp

- The Extension Alliance for Better Child Care offers adaptations and modifications for children in early childhood settings that are useful to the pre-K classroom. Detailed supports are given for children with a variety of abilities, learning and social-emotional needs, visual and hearing needs, and physical needs: https://childcare. extension.org/adapting-the-child-care-envi ronment-for-children-with-special-needs

Writing Personalized Supports

In a lesson plan, individualization explains how the teacher will support learning or adapt materials to strengthen learning and developmental skills specific children will use during activities. For example, a teacher may need to support one child with the use of scissors (a physical skill) or scaffold interactions with peers (a social-emotional skill).

It is helpful to create a chart with the skill listed on the left and the desired goal for a child on the right. What skill comes with ease as a child masters an activity? What skill is emerging? What skill remains challenging or is lagging behind other areas of development? Answers can be written in a notebook as you notice daily challenges and successes. The goal will state what you want the child to be able to do with increasing competence. For example, "Jonah will be able to hang his coat independently."

While goals may be taken from individualized education program (IEP) documents, it is up to you to individualize and adjust the kind of support you give to help children achieve goals. Goals are equally important for children with strong skills—to identify new areas of challenge or to address inconsistencies. Children in pre-K need a lot of support in group settings. Adaptations can be written for about a quarter of children each week, ensuring that each month, all receive updated and individualized support. However, the total number in each lesson plan depends on the specific needs of each child.

Importantly, goals should build on the unique strengths of each child and offer support that ensures well-being and positive development. Figure 4.1 offers some sample goals that are individualized for specific children.

Sample Individualized Goals

Child and Goal	Standard	Individualization and Support
Cameron Goal: Play cooperatively with peers during play with increasing independence.	2.0/2.1: More actively and intentionally cooperate with peers.	Introduce board game with noncompetitive goal (e.g., collecting nuts for squirrel nest). Use individual spinners and standing table. Begin games with adult assistance. Offer gradually decreasing social support.
Lucas Goal: Copy name independently.	1.3: Write first name nearly correctly.	Offer a variety of play-based writing practice games with letter samples. Model and scaffold skills. Monday, foam writing. Tuesday, sand writing. Wednesday, large pencils and trace letters. Thursday, markers and whiteboard. Friday, lined paper and pencil.
Sabiyah Goal: Engage with and explore picture books with increasing independence.	5.1: Demonstrate enjoyment of literacy and literacy-related activities.	Respond to Sabiyah's interest and compile a group of books about horses in a portable basket. Engage in small group and one-on-one reading. Offer books for home reading.
Eleanor Goal: Participate and remain engaged during group reading activity.	3.1: Participate positively and cooperate as group members.	Offer lap pets to hold. Sit next to Ms. Noni. Use laminated picture cards as answer choices to use during partner turn and talk activities.
Celeth Goal: Use words to ask for help during social interactions with peers.	2.1: Regulate their attention, thoughts, feelings, and impulses more consistently, although adult guidance is sometimes necessary.	Use feelings chart with puppets. Reinforce request phrases like "No, thank you," "Need help," "Please, may I?" and "I want to . . ." Increase observation and supervision for earlier support in social situations.

Figure 4.1. Demonstrates how to individualize goals for children. (Standards from CDE [2008].)

Making the Most of Learning Objectives

Ms. Carmen finishes reading *Snowmen at Night,* by Caralyn Buehner. She asks, "What would you do if you were a snowman at night?" Zeke says, "I'd drink hot chocolate and sit in a hot tub!" Lorena says, "I'd do skating tricks on ice. And have a snowball fight." "I'd do a wild ride down the hill," says Charlie. "Oh, that's very scary," says Lorena. Ms. Carmen agrees. "You are right, Lorena. These activities are a big thrill. A *thrill* is a favorite activity you do that is exciting. But it shouldn't be scary if a grownup is with you."

Ms. Carmen holds up large photos of children enjoying winter sports. "Let's look at some thrilling activities. What is this child doing?" Anderson replies. "He's playing hockey." "That's right. For hockey, children try to slide the puck into the net with a stick. And what is this child doing?" Anderson says, "Skiing," Ms. Carmen elaborates, "Yes, skiing is a way of getting down the hill using poles and long skis attached to your boots. When you ski, you use your poles to balance. What about this child?" Lorena answers, "He's pulling a sled." Ms. Carmen says, "Yes, do you see him holding on tight to the rope? It looks like he's pulling his little sister. What is this?" The children are not sure. Ms. Carmen tells them, "It's a snowboard. A snowboard looks like a skateboard. You have to work hard to balance while you slide." While pointing to the photos, Ms. Carmen says, "Ice hockey, sledding, skiing, and snowboarding are winter sports. These are activities we can enjoy when it is cold and snowy outside."

Ms. Carmen wants the children to be able to retell stories and compare activities. These children live in a warm climate and do not know much about snow and winter sports. Some of the children have never seen or felt snow. In addition to providing books and stories, Ms. Carmen has created a memory game in which the children will match pictures of winter sports.

Ms. Carmen has clear learning objectives. She wants the children to understand how weather can make more work for people and it can create opportunities for play. She has created a sorting activity where the children must decide if the weather has created work or play. When cars get muddy, sand gets in the house, the wind blows yard furniture over, or rain gets clothes wet, this can make more work. When snow falls or it's a bright sunny day, there are many ways for children to play.

During these activities, the children will learn many basic facts: that weather changes, that different seasons bring different weather patterns, and that weather impacts people's clothing and activities. They learn these facts about weather in the context of much more complex ideas. They will be able to do much more than identify sunny, windy, snowy, and rainy day and know how to dress for the weather. Ms. Carmen wants the children to be deep thinkers and to consider why meteorologists are important and how people can prepare for and benefit from weather patterns.

As you review your state's early learning guidelines, choose direct teaching, mini-lessons, and shared learning as strategies to introduce new topics and information. You may identify one or more learning objectives you want to teach and support. Below are five kinds of learning objectives:

1. **Content objectives:** Are there facts, concepts, relationships, or sequences of events children are to explore? What knowledge do you want children to be able to understand and communicate about this topic or concept? What vocabulary will children need to talk about their ideas? How does this knowledge relate to other concepts? Are there specific language, reading, writing, math, science, social studies, or socio-cultural facts children need to know or understanding they need to have in order to compete this activity? Do children need to listen, speak, discuss, write, or represent ideas? Do they need to explore books to find information?

2. **Skill objectives:** Are there procedures or problem-solving steps you want children to complete? Are there physical skills, such as manipulating or creating involved? Do children need to use strategies, organize work, or follow directions? Do they need to use tools or equipment? Can they carry out expectations and procedures?

3. **Language objectives:** Language for learning involves different words and meanings than everyday language. Do children understand the procedural language needed to complete an activity? Academic language is conveyed as part of Bloom's taxonomy, such as *identify*, *label*, *list*, *describe*, *discuss*, *apply*, *predict*, *compare*, *create*, *choose*, *estimate*, and *evaluate*. Children may not understand words like *demonstrate*, *explain*, and *review*. Have you modeled these concepts so that children know what to do?

4. **Behavior objectives.** Consider the skills children need to transition in and out of an activity, self-monitor, socialize, and problem solve. Are there other aspects of executive function required, such as shifting attention, focusing, and flexibility? Do children need to interact appropriately with others?

5. **Higher-level thinking objectives.** What critical thinking skills do you want children to use? What more complex ideas do you want them to understand? How will you demonstrate and explain these in a way that makes sense to the children? Do you want them to explain, predict, evaluate, or compare?

HELPFUL HINT

Being Proactive

As you focus on preparing and implementing lesson plans, small adjustments can have big impact. Here are some great tips to ensure everything goes as you intend.

Double check needed materials for each lesson. What materials or props will you need to read, model, or demonstrate? What resources (web, books, learning materials, games) will you use to carry out your goals? What technology (if any) will you need? List any references or resources you use for activities or materials so these can be used again.

When you are completely finished with your lesson plan, update your materials list. You may have forgotten to include scissors, tape, or paper. A complete list of items will keep you from scrambling at the last minute or making children wait. You'll be able to collect, arrange, and introduce activities much more easily with a complete list.

Plan directions. Rather than remind children of directions once they get started, rehearse directions before the activity begins, and give a list of printed steps or sequential pictures for needed steps in procedures. Use picture cards, including signs for agree and disagree or who talks and who listens.

Review and rehearse steps that will be needed for procedures. Rehearsing can include walking through the steps to practice and/or having students explain the expectations back to you.

Keep children active. Be sure no one is just sitting during teacher-directed activities. All children can answer questions on a white board. Give children clipboards or personal white boards so that all children can represent their thinking, plan an activity, or answer questions using words, marks, drawings, or pictures.

Be realistic about time. Often a "single" lesson plan actually needs a week to complete! You may plan one learning goal that will need a sequence of teacher-directed (and child-responsive) activities to achieve. Be careful not to overload one lesson.

Aim for mini-lessons. Rather than teach big chunks of information that require elaborate steps, keep the time children are required to attend to your teaching very brief. Presenting smaller mini-lessons is often much more effective than presenting a single extended teaching segment. Over the pre-K year, children will begin to engage for longer periods of time, especially as they enjoy group book reading and lively interactive conversations.

Rehearse book reading or modeled activities. You may find a book reading session requires more time than you planned or that there are important questions you can ask to boost engagement. You may discover that an activity doesn't work out like a website describes or find you need more time or materials. Run through the steps to be sure.

Maximizing Vocabulary in Content Areas

Children love to express themselves and play with sounds and rhymes. They still enjoy finger plays and hand movements that emphasize rhymes in songs and chants. They take pride in learning new words. Every daily informal and formal interaction provides an opportunity to emphasize word meanings and to enrich children's understanding of vocabulary. Books are the perfect source of new words and concepts. Conversations during outdoor play, transitions, and meals also offer rich teaching moments for introducing vocabulary. The following are some practical ways to make language meaningful as children learn about content areas:

> **Pre-teach vocabulary.** When introducing vocabulary words, do so before you read a book rather than during the book reading. Teaching vocabulary ahead of time creates a perfect introduction to a book, its concepts, and characters. Describe the word meaning by relating it to words and ideas the children already know. Pre-teaching vocabulary creates an engaging moment when children joyfully recognize the new words within the story. During reading, point to illustrations that show the word meaning. Encourage children to use the new words when answering questions.

> **Include culturally relevant vocabulary.** Use books and materials that reflect the racial, ethnic, linguistic, and economic diversity present in your program. Include daily events, situations, and settings that present families and neighborhoods that are familiar. Use words with pictures and label items in children's home languages. For example, in Spanish: book/*el libro*, march/*la marcha*, shopping/ *de compras*, shopping bag/*bolsa de la compra*, family/*familia*. Ask the children to pronounce words. They take pride in sharing their knowledge and expertise. For dual language learners, interactive word walls are a literacy tool that assists them with reading and writing (Fountas & Pinell, 2010) (Figure 4.2). They include the letters of the alphabet and a space to display words across a wall in the main area of the classroom. At first, young children may help you add their names to the word wall in alphabetical order. Later, you can involve them in adding words that you have selected and words that come from children's interests and needs.

> **Use picture maps and graphic organizers.** Picture maps organize children's ideas and help them see how things relate. They can contribute facts and ideas and then group them into like categories. For example, collies, poodles, and beagles are kinds of dogs. Dogs, cats, fish, and gerbils are animals we care for as pets. This kind of learning starts with specific examples that generate a big idea or concept. On the other hand, if you ask, "How do we help our families?" the learning can start with the big concept of helping and then children generate specific examples. For example, helping includes putting away clothes and bringing a diaper to baby brother.

> **Encourage small group storytelling.** Ask children to make up and retell stories (Flynn 2016). To encourage storytelling, ask children to explain their artwork. Ask them to tell stories about family experiences. Invite children to make up alternative endings to books you have read together. Brainstorm fanciful tales where characters do impossible things. Write a group story on a large paper chart and children contribute "what happened next" sentences. Storytelling is a wonderful way to learn about children and share the joy of writing and communicating.

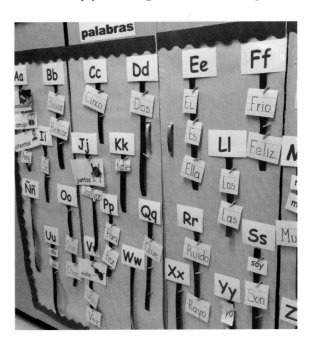

Figure 4.2. Example of an interactive word wall. (Reprinted from Alanís, I., Arreguín M., & Salinas González, I. 2021. *The Essentials: Supporting Dual Language Learners in Diverse Environments in Preschool and Kindergarten*. Washington, DC: NAEYC.)

> **Move from rote to robust.** When you ask questions, consider whether the answer you desire invites more than one correct response. Ask questions in a way that invites many ideas and answers. For example, instead of "Where does a hat go?," ask "Why do people need to keep their heads warm?" Children's answers may include: "So our ears don't freeze," or "So we don't get cold." Or ask, "How do we cover and protect our heads?" Children may have many ideas: "We can wrap a scarf around our head," "We can wear a hat," and "My coat has a hood that flips up." In this way, children are exposed to many ideas and learn from their peers as well as from you. When asked open-ended questions over time, children experience hundreds of opportunities to learn from each other and to think more deeply about topics, concepts, and related vocabulary.

> **Follow children's interests.** Children are curious about the world around them. They frequently ask why things happen in the world. They are eager to see, listen to, taste, touch, and smell objects they encounter. As you help them investigate their environment to discover how and why processes occur, you can use informational books and conversations to introduce new vocabulary, critical thinking questions, and ideas.

Sample Lesson Plans
Teacher-Directed Learning

As you consider how to provide increasing challenge and opportunities for deeper learning, don't try everything all at once. Start with your current lesson plan and build on it. The idea is to recognize that all lessons can be enhanced and children can discover meaningful and engaging ways to learn throughout the day. First steps include the following:

> Begin by choosing a group of books that highlight a thematic concept. Group these together in a basket or on a shelf and display several with colorful covers.

> Choose content standards and write the big ideas you want to teach. Add key vocabulary.

> Create a simple introduction that gives children visual, hands-on, and creative ways to become curious about and involved in the topic. Ask questions that connect new ideas and content to their current experiences.

> Write questions to ask children during shared book reading. Insert the cards in the pages of the book or keep them ready to use.

> Demonstrate a new concept, skill, or realistic (hands-on) learning activity. Ask children to reenact this during a table activity or in a learning/play area.

> Integrate vocabulary and concepts into play areas. Write prompt cards as a reminder to introduce or revisit ideas, questions, and investigations during play.

> Hold a brainstorm session with your coteacher to review the materials in your classroom. For the lesson below, consider featuring a vegetable or fruit each day. Focus on farming and how food comes to the table (e.g., *Before We Eat: From Farm to Table,* by Pat Brisson). Your goal is to introduce and facilitate increasingly more complex thinking about new ideas and concepts to lead children's learning forward.

While the lesson in Figure 4.3 can be conducted outdoors for programs that have container or ground gardens, programs located in the city can also develop indoor container and salad gardens. The focus of the lesson is to connect children to the sources of their food, to discover that food production is remarkable, and to develop a lifelong interest in healthy food sources.

Sample Lesson Plans

Title/Topic of Lesson: Growing a Garden

Date: April 15

Materials

> **Books, props, materials, games:** *From Seed to Plant*, by Gail Gibbons; prepared tray; plant sequencing cards; gourds and seed pods; cucumber, apple, and green pepper; knife and cutting board; foil to line the windowsill.

> Prepare trays that contain one of each of the following for each child:

- Baggies of potting soil (one cup each)
- Lettuce seeds
- Plastic fork
- Cut clear plastic soda bottle bottom (pot)
- Science journal and pencil

Also provide several small watering cans, filled, with sprinkle spouts.

> **Web resources, technology:** Smartboard for bean time-lapse sprouting video (www.youtube.com/watch?v=w77zPAtVTuI) and spinach time-lapse sprouting video (www.youtube.com/watch?v=sMK-BKUYMOs).

> **Practical tools (e.g., paper, scissors, tape):** Magnifying glasses, paper towels, spray bottles with water

Book List

Before We Eat: From Farm to Table, by Pat Brisson

Eating the Alphabet, by Lois Ehlert

Farming, by Gail Gibbons

From Seed to Pumpkin, by Wendy Pfeffer

Growing Vegetable Soup, by Lois Ehlert

Planting a Rainbow, by Lois Ehlert

Right This Very Minute: A Table-To-Farm Book About Food and Farming, by Lisl H. Detlefsen

The Tiny Seed, by Eric Carle

The Vegetables We Eat, by Gail Gibbons

Standards

1. **List of standards.** 3.B.ECa: Identify basic similarities and differences in pictures and information. 2.B.3c: Ask and answer questions about book read aloud. 5.8ECa: Use drawing, dictating, or writing to express ideas about a topic. 10.A.ECa: Ask meaningful questions that can be answered through gathering information. 10.B.ECb: Make predictions about what will happen next. 11.A.ECc: Plan and carry out simple investigations. 12.A.ECa: Observe, investigate, describe, and categorize living things.

2. **Learning goals (big ideas, concept learning).**

> People take care of gardens and orchards to produce food and flowers.

> Plants and growing things depend on soil, sun, and water to grow.

> While gardening involves plants, dirt, digging, and watering, many other creatures grow in a garden. The garden hosts and needs insects and animals (e.g., worms keep the earth soft, butterflies drink from the flowers, bees pollinate flowers and vegetables, bugs and insects eat leaves, spiders are present to eat insects).

> Things change over time (e.g., seasons, weather, plant growth, cycles of caring for gardens).

3. **Content and academic vocabulary.** Content words: *botanist, cactus, holes, nutrient, perennial, roots, seeds, soil, sprout, thrive.* Academic words: *compare, experiment, observe, record.*

4. **Introduction/anticipatory set.**

> Basket of gourds and seed pods to shake and listen. Questions: What do you think is making the sound? How did the seeds get inside? (When gourds and seed pods dry, the seeds become loose inside. All fruits grow seeds inside.)

> Apple, cucumber, and green pepper to cut, revealing seeds. Questions: What are seeds? Where are seeds? (Seeds are planted in the ground to make plants grow. Seeds grow inside some plants that grow from the ground. People save the seeds and plant them. One fruit has many seeds).

5. **Teaching activity. Read the book *From Seed to Plant*, by Gail Gibbons.**

Questions:

> What is growing in our classroom garden? (flowers, parsley)

> What is growing in our yard? (trees, bushes, plants, flowers)

> What kind of plants do your families grow? (food, flowers, plants, bushes)

> What is happening in this picture? (the plant is growing)

> What do you think is hiding inside the bag? (seeds, dirt, plants)

> When water is poured on the seed, does it grow right away? How long will it take for the seeds to sprout? (from a few days to a few weeks)

> In the book, the lady grew bean sprouts. We are going to grow lettuce. What will our lettuce seeds need to sprout? (a container, soil, sun)

Demonstration: Model how to pour dirt into bottle pots. Rake the soil with fork. Poke holes in soil with back of fork. Sprinkle seeds. Water with watering can. Ask children to describe and draw the planting of the seeds. Over time, they will draw the continued growth of the plant.

Notes: Ask coteacher to distribute materials. Assist children in planting seeds. Place seed pots on windowsill lined with foil to protect the sill.

6. **Extend learning concepts into play area activities and child-centered activities.**

> **Reading and language:** *Eating the Alphabet*, by Lois Ehlert. Phonemic awareness and phonics focus on beginning word sounds. Laminate matching uppercase and lowercase letters A–K to match with fruit and vegetable photos at fine motor table. Place book copy in listening library.

> **Dramatic play:** Farm stand theme materials: Small vegetable containers and baskets, chalk- or white board to write prices, garden gloves, watering cans/pails, clipboards with attached pens for drawing (planning) a garden, cash register and money, shopping carts or boxes (shoebox size), aprons and sunhats. Prepare dirt table with garden gloves, pots, plant containers, rakes, trowels, and plastic seeds and worms.

> **Mathematics/fine motor:** (1) Graph the number of trees and bushes in the school, roof, or courtyard. Graph favorite fruits and vegetables. (2) Counting seeds in seed packets (real or teacher-generated). (3) Teacher-generated board game: How many worms in my garden? Roll counting cubes or dice to add two numbers and help the worms wiggle their way across the garden. (4) Matching number cards (numerals and dots to number of plants/vegetables).

> **Science/Nature:** Matching card sort (tree, flower, plant, vegetables) depicting seed, sprout, rooted small plant, and mature plant for children to sequence. Farming and plant puzzles. Examine various seeds (e.g., beans) with magnifying glass.

> **Social skills/Self-regulation:** Responsibility for classroom (watering plants). Taking responsibility for toys and belongings. Following steps in a project.

> **Sand and water:** Watering cans, gardening tools, insects, and bugs.

> **Visual arts:** Painting flowers and vegetables.

> **Music and movement:** Sing the following verses to the tune of "The Farmer in the Dell": (1) the gardener plants the seeds, (2) the sun comes up to shine, (3) the rain begins to fall, (4) the flower begins to bloom, and (5) the plant begins to grow.

7. **Observing and documenting children's learning.**

Name:	Date:
Learning Goals	**Observation Notes**
Children will follow simple directions to plant seeds. Children will be able to explain what happens when they plant a seed. Children will explain what is needed for a seed to grow.	Sequenced steps in plant growth using picture cards. Expressed ideas about planting.
Questions	**Child's Responses**
1. Where do seeds grow? (e.g., in the ground, inside pods, fruit) 2. What happens when seeds are planted? 3. What do seeds need in order to grow? (How do you take care of your seeds?)	

8. Individualization and support.

Physical skills: Manipulate pots, soil, seeds, and watering can.

Regulation: Remember and follow directions.

Note: This lesson plan provides general skills and modifications for individualization. You may provide these for specific children as needed.

Physical modifications:

> Secure plastic pot to table with tape to prevent sliding.

> Provide funnels to assist with pouring soil.

> Provide alternative pegs with grips to poke holes for seeds.

> Provide gloves to protect hands.

> Offer standing as well as sitting tables.

> Ensure adequate space.

Regulation modifications:

> Provide picture cards with steps in sequence.

> Ensure play areas are prepared for subsequent activity, so children do not have to wait when the current activity is complete.

Child and Goal	Standard	Individualization and Support
Jillian Goal: Participate in conversations to express ideas and understanding.	2.B.3c: Ask and answer questions about book read aloud.	Ask questions during individual book reading about gardening with alternative ways to answer (point to painting, journal, or book illustrations)
Paul Goal: Sequence events over time.	3.B.ECa: Identify basic similarities and differences in pictures and information.	Work one-on-one to support Paul in sequencing steps of plant growth using larger-sized pictures.
Serina Goal: Engage in painting or art activity.	5.8ECa: Use drawing, dictating, or writing to express ideas about a topic.	Provide gloves and alternative brushes (larger size, with grips) and offer painting at table in addition to easel.

9. Adaptations during teacher-directed or child-centered activities.

10. Family connections: Share book list. Encourage families to sprout new plants from the ends of onions, celery, carrots, lettuce, and garlic. Ask families to bring children to the grocery store or market and identify two vegetables and two fruits. Which is the smallest (largest)? What are the colors? Ask children to draw what they see.

11. Notes (what worked well, what to change next time): Use this space to record what worked well and what needs to be changed or improved.

Figure 4.3. Demonstrates a gardening theme that shows children where healthy foods come from. (Standards from Illinois State Board of Education [2013].)

Standard 3—Teaching includes the purposeful use of multiple instructional approaches to optimize children's opportunities for learning. Teachers use a range of approaches from structured to unstructured and from adult directed to child directed. Standard 3.G requires that instruction deepens children's understanding and their skills and knowledge. Teachers create experiences that engage children in purposeful and meaningful learning. You'll need a deep knowledge of content and methods for teaching, along with understanding of children's developmental needs and skills. You must be able to develop lesson plans that

> Provide children with opportunities to engage in group projects (Standard 3D.5)

> Provide children with opportunities to learn from one another (3D.6)

> Change materials and events over a period of months (3D.8)

Standard 3.E addresses the many ways teachers can use and rearrange the classroom, materials, and activities to meet the needs of specific children and promote engagement in learning. You'll encourage children to ask questions, connect to prior knowledge, and extend their understanding and interest in the world. An important aspect of effective teaching is the need to adequately challenge children. You can break down larger skills into meaningful and achievable parts. This level of intentionality and planning is essential to your effective classroom teaching.

REFLECTION QUESTIONS

1. What do you enjoy most about your current teacher-directed lesson planning? Why do you feel this way?

2. What first steps would you like to take to enhance your teacher-directed activities?

3. What can you add to your current lesson plans that will make a difference in the effectiveness of your teaching?

CHAPTER 5

Using Observation, Documentation, and Assessment to Guide Teaching

Understanding Assessment with Young Children

After reading *Rosie Revere, Engineer,* by Andrea Beaty, the children are excited to build their own structures. Ms. Kelsey watches Noah fit together two curved wooden train tracks. He tries to slide the tracks underneath a bridge, but the block structure crumbles. Noah unhooks the tracks and rebuilds the structure. He selects two straight pieces of track and connects them together under the bridge. "Yay! My bridge stayed up! I got some cool engineering skills."

Ms. Kelsey says, "Noah, you are a hardworking builder. You used your engineering skills to solve a problem. How did you fix it?" Noah responds, "The straight track fit. The curved track was too tight. I put the bridge up. Then I put the tracks in." Ms. Kelsey responds, "That was good planning. You made the opening bigger so the straight tracks fit. May I take a photo?" Noah nods.

Ms. Kelsey snaps a photo of the bridge and captures Noah's grin at the same time.

She prints the photo and writes the caption. "A straight track can fit, but the curved track is too tight. I put the bridge up. Then I put the track in." She adds, "Engineer _____" and hands the clipboard to Noah. He slowly prints his name in the blank space she has left. Ms. Kelsey smiles and says, "Engineer Noah. You have some cool engineering skills."

Ms. Kelsey uses assessment as an integrated part of teaching. She documents the insight that Noah has about his problem-solving strategy. Noah clips his photograph to the learning line. Ms. Kelsey writes three vocabulary words to use tomorrow: *curves*, *corners*, and *connections*. These concepts will expand Noah's thinking and communication about his favorite activity. She uses observation and documentation to evaluate and understand Noah's skills and needs.

Assessment measures the change in what children know and can do over time. Assessment provides essential information that shows you what children understand. It is part of everyday teaching and takes place in multiple forms and situations.

Assessment helps you answer questions like "Where are children in their learning progress?," "Do they need support to deepen their understanding?," "Are there skills that need support?," and "Do they need additional challenge to keep pace with their skills?"

Before writing a lesson plan, you'll need to decide the best way to document what children are learning. Once you know your options, you can choose the assessment type that makes sense for the kind of activity you are planning. You'll be able to write lesson plans more quickly and accurately capture how children's skills are progressing.

TIPS FOR TEACHING

Exploring and
Using Data

There are many forms of evidence that show children are learning. Data are needed to document how children are making progress and to show whether your teaching choices are effective. Sometimes, you will collect evidence that includes quantitative (or numerical) information; for example

> How many objects did a child count?

> How many animals did a child identify?

> How many activities did a child complete successfully?

> How many letter sounds did the child say correctly?

Quantitative data show progress toward specific skills. For example, when you collect samples of children's work over a period of time, you can answer questions like "How many more letters can a child write in December than in September?" and "How many shape attributes can a child accurately describe?"

However, with young children, the most useful data often are qualitative. Qualitative (or descriptive) data include a rich and detailed written record or evidence that captures what you observe. Examples of descriptive data that can help you make effective teaching choices include when you

> Identify emerging skills

> Describe specific strengths and competencies

> Communicate what children know and can do

> Explain how children are learning and what works well for them

> Evaluate whether children have accomplished specific goals during an activity or experience

> Record how children's skills are more advanced than last week

> Detail areas of learning or development that need support

> Document materials and activities children need to develop new skills

> Keep track of ways children have gained competence

Understanding the Assessment Cycle

Ms. Nikki watches Vallie and Jack at the fine motor table. Vallie works carefully to peel a strip of paper from the tip of a carpenter's pencil to reveal more of the red waxy center. She uses it to draw a large square on graph paper. Then, she reaches for a magnetic block.

Jack taps Vallie's arm and says, "Let's make a picnic for the animals." Vallie considers this option. "Okay. We can make a picnic shelter." Ms. Nikki says, "A shelter will protect the animals from the rain." Vallie says, "Their mothers will bring a raincoat and umbrella." Ms. Nikki agrees. "That's right. The raincoat and umbrella provide protection too." Vallie adds, "They won't get wet."

This looks like a typical interaction, but Ms. Nikki is observing Vallie's play activity to evaluate her fine motor and communication skills. The children learned the words *shelter* and *protection* when Ms. Nikki read *Down Comes the Rain,* by Franklyn M. Branley, and *What Will the Weather Be?* by Lynda DeWitt. She introduces these concepts during the children's play.

Ms. Nikki writes the date and details on her clipboard: "Vallie was persistent and peeled paper from the pencil. She shifted her focus when Jack suggested making a picnic for the animals. She used *shelter* in a sentence. Vallie knew that a raincoat and umbrella give protection."

The goal of assessment is to identify each child's strengths and emerging skills and to clarify areas of development or learning that need additional support. Assessment will help you

> Evaluate whether children are developing skills according to typical or expected timeframes

> Consider which areas of development are advancing and which need additional support

> Select new or more complex materials and activities for additional learning

> Identify adaptations and modifications of materials for individual children

> Adjust levels of support, challenge, and stimulation for creative experiences and learning

> Enrich interactions to provide focused language support

> Reflect on teaching practices to be more linguistically and culturally relevant

> Evaluate the level of challenge or complexity to stimulate children's growth

> Consider specific skills needed for children to engage successfully with materials

> Modify spaces, materials, timing, and level of support to ensure behavior success

> Share information with families so they can collaborate to strengthen children's skills

> Assessment and planning processes are part of the same evaluation cycle. Well-planned assessment helps you take into consideration the context of children's experience that impacts their adjustment and growth. Figure 5.1 shows the evaluation cycle you will follow.

Evaluation Cycle

Figure 5.1. Evaluation Cycle. Assessment for learning uses this five-part evaluation cycle.

Observation

Observation is the intentional and deliberate exploration of all present factors that impact children's learning. As you observe, you notice the way children behave, respond, and learn in relationship to the setting and materials. You pay attention to how children interact with their peers. You note how children respond during their interactions with you. You evaluate how the level of support, the time frame or schedule, and the child's physical or emotional state impact their adjustment, engagement, and learning.

When you observe, you also keep track of what and how children learn. Do they have conversations that include new vocabulary? Do they demonstrate understanding of concepts during play? Do they follow directions or carry out needed procedures with increasing independence? Do they demonstrate needed skills? Are there areas of learning that are frustrating to the child? The goal of observation is to gather a variety of evidence that helps you know children well, identify strengths and needs, and plan effective teaching.

Documentation

Documentation means capturing in fair and accurate ways what you have seen and heard. There are many ways to document what you observe. You will capture evidence of learning through observational notes or by using developmental checklists to describe emerging skills. You will create portfolios to hold examples of children's artwork, drawing, dictation, and other learning evidence. Realistic documentation can include photographs, artwork, video recordings, journals, and other dimensional products created by children. Each type of evidence adds to a complete and meaningful picture of children's development and learning.

Reflection

Reflection invites insight into the specific needs of each child. What does this child do well? What else will challenge his or her thinking and growth? What other materials and conversations can you introduce to develop specific skills? Are your interactions, messages, and ways of support effective in motivating this child? You will consider areas in which this child struggles or needs encouragement and support.

What books or resources will add to the strength of an interest? What can you prepare, arrange, adjust, or do differently that will engage this child in more meaningful learning?

Adapting Strategies

Adapting strategies means you use what you have learned to teach more effectively. You may realize that support is needed in fine or gross motor skills. You can plan additional games, add physical props, and modify materials. You may find that a child needs encouragement to engage in book reading or that you want to focus more intentionally on supporting vocabulary development. You may want to provide scaffolding for peer interactions. Your goal is always to strengthen children's competence and perception of themselves as capable, active learners.

Assessing Learning

Assessing learning means that you develop a deep and complex understanding of children and what they know and can do. Commercial assessments are linked to a specific curriculum or skill checklists. Authentic, program-specific assessments determine where children are in the sequence of learning and the extent to which they have achieved desired learning objectives and goals. You will use a variety of assessment strategies, which ensure a full and accurate picture of children's progress in the moment and over time.

RESEARCH CONNECTIONS

Identifying Equity Issues

Assessment serves four purposes, including monitoring children's development and learning, guiding curriculum planning and decision making, identifying children with disabilities, and obtaining accurate information to share with families, colleagues, and other stakeholders (Ntuli, Nyarambi, & Traore 2014). Within each purpose, careful attention must be given to ensure equity, fairness, and support for children with disabilities, children of color, children and families who are immigrants or refugees, and children who are multilingual learners (Carley Rizzuto 2018; Chu & Flores 2011).

The goal of assessment is always to strengthen children's well-being, development, capabilities, knowledge, skills, and abilities. Teachers must be aware of sensitive issues when evaluating children.

> Young children's language and early literacy skills are just emerging, yet many evaluations rely on language capability. Children need opportunities to "show" their skills rather than "tell" what they know (McConnell 2019).

> Children's development is rapid and inconsistent. An evaluation on one day or at one time does not provide an accurate picture of a child's overall progress (Schultz 2015).

> Children are developing thinking processes and ways to reflect on learning. It is as important to understand how children are learning as to determine what they know (Salmon 2016).

> Evaluation of children must consider children's perspectives. Teachers must think about the influence of the social and physical setting and use reflective practice to be sure they have an accurate view (Buzzelli 2018).

> Commercial assessments should be evaluated to ensure the content is suited for children from varied racial and income groups and for children learning multiple languages (Wood & Schatschneider 2019).

> Teachers should use multiple sources of information to evaluate children who are multilingual learners and use caution when interpreting vocabulary assessments (Wood & Schatschneider 2019).

> Teachers should exercise caution when using rating scales of children's academic performance and behavior. Teachers' judgments of children can be impacted by stereotypes and bias stemming from cultural differences (Mason, Gunersel, & Ney 2014).

> Ratings of children's learning and behavior are influenced by teacher attitudes, beliefs, and previous experiences, including a cultural mismatch between children and the teacher (Rudd 2014; Staats 2014). Reflection and honest appraisal are essential.

> When kindergarten readiness assessments are required, these should be used to identify gaps in learning and to plan for more effective teaching (Regenstein et al. 2017). Readiness assessments "should be designed appropriately for the population being evaluated, including being culturally and linguistically responsive, and developed based on the intended purposes of the assessment" (5).

Benefiting from Authentic Assessment

"So, you have a new bedroom?" asks Ms. Rian when Teagan swallows a bite of muffin. "Yes. I got a bunk bed. Mamma made me sleep on the bottom," says Teagan. "Would you rather sleep on the top bunk?" asks Ms. Rian. "Well, my animals might fall off." "Hmm," says Ms. Rian. "I think your animals and you will be very cozy sleeping on the bottom. Who sleeps with you?" "My giraffe and panda," answers Teagan with a grin. "I am glad you will all be safe," smiles Ms. Rian.

Ms. Rian connects with Teagan daily at lunch. Teagan's dad is on an extended trip and Teagan has a new baby brother. Teagan is seeing a speech therapist once a week. During meals, Ms. Rian tunes in to Tegan's progress. She takes note of Teagan's sense of humor and her full-sentence answers. Ms. Rian uses informal lunchtime conversations to keep track of Teagan's progress.

Authentic assessment evaluates children during the course of normal activities with familiar routines and teachers. This approach ensures an accurate picture of children's skills, thinking, and abilities. It involves observing children in multiple ways, times, and places. Authentic assessment evaluates how children respond to many experiences and situations.

During authentic assessment, you engage children in conversation, ask them to demonstrate or explain what they know, or simply observe them during an activity. The goal is to capture a meaningful picture of progress when the child is comfortable. Children may not be aware that their progress is being assessed.

Observe and document what children do in at least three ways. One way is to observe what children can do independently. For example, watch how children match domino numbers and then ask follow-up questions about their thinking. Another way is to evaluate what children can do during shared activities with you. For example, when reading a book, keep track of what children say about a story or record their answers to questions. Also, observe and document what children do and say during interactions with their peers. For example, you may notice the way children solve problems or manage social situations. Watching and evaluating in many contexts gives you a complete picture.

Authentic assessment ensures needed information is gathered

> About what children know and can do

> About children's progress over time

> To prepare materials, plan time, and make decisions

The purpose of authentic assessment is to identify each child's strengths and emerging skills and to clarify areas that need additional support. This information can be shared with families so that they can participate in encouraging and fostering children's strengths. You will use assessment information to plan specific materials, activities, adaptations, modifications, and other supports for individual children. The following statements explain how authentic assessment works:

Authentic assessment is ongoing. The process of evaluating children involves many times, many places, and many ways to capture what children know and can do. Authentic assessment ensures that you have looked at children in many situations. Rather than making decisions based on one morning or one day, you look for patterns over time.

Authentic assessment is cyclical. Authentic assessment information helps you reflect on and adapt your own practices. Teachers engage in a predictable sequence of steps that include observation, reflection, adaptation, and fine-tuning practice to meet the needs of children. This use of

assessment is called *formative assessment*, and you use your insight and understanding gained from it to adapt the level of support, stimulation, creative experience, and approaches to teaching. You continue to adapt your practice to ensure the most effective teaching decisions.

Authentic assessment requires you to ask the right questions. When finding out what children know and understand, you must use questions and activities that make sense to the child. You can consider "What does this child do well?," "What else can I do to strengthen his or her thinking and growth?," "In what areas does this child struggle or need encouragement?," and "How can I introduce materials, conversation, activities, and books that connect to the child's current understanding and build additional strengths?"

Authentic assessment provides information for individualization. Individualized support for learning is a central part of evaluation. It involves using what is learned about children to plan future materials, activities, and interactions. Individualized teaching does not simply address areas of weakness or skills that are not yet present. The purpose is to identify emerging skills and continue to develop strengths in each area of development.

Authentic assessment requires unbiased documentation. Accurate and unbiased observation means that adults record what is observed in objective and unemotional terms. Rather than say, "Bryon struggled with nap transition today," an accurate report would say, "Bryon cried during nap transition. He was sad that Jackson had to go home. We talked about how happy he would feel when Jackson returns next week." That accurate version takes into consideration what is happening around the child that contributes to a situation. Often, teacher choices, actions, or events have contributed to the way a child responds.

The goal of assessment is to capture the timing and sequence of skills as they emerge in the context of consistent support and encouragement from teachers. Teachers strengthen children's skill or comprehension level by having one-on-one conversations, modeling skills, and providing support and encouragement. Assessment with young children does not always aim to capture what they can do alone, but it also includes what children can do with support.

Exploring Types of Authentic Assessment

Types of authentic assessment include observational notes, developmental checklists (which may be commercial assessment tools to measure children's emerging skills and progress), portfolios, rating scales, and other realistic documentation. Teachers can choose the kind of assessment that fits most naturally with the daily routine, the activity, and the child. The use of each kind of assessment must be matched carefully to its purpose. It must also be used in combination with other kinds of evaluation and documentation. The information below introduces the purpose and approach of each type of assessment tool.

Writing Observational Notes and Anecdotal Records

> Aimee tries to fit the veterinarian tools back into the kit. She is frustrated because it won't latch. She takes out the reflex hammer, turns it around, and shuts the case. Jonathan interrupts her and says, "Help me. My puppy got run over with a bike. He's crying." Aimee looks up, opens the kit, and takes out a bandage. "I am sorry your puppy hurt his foot. Here is a bandage to fix his leg." She and Jonathan work hard to get the bandage to stay on. "Thank you. He's better now," says Jonathan.

Ms. Kia has been keeping track of Aimee over the past week. She's trying to get a good picture about her intense focus and how this relates to her learning. She makes a chart to take observational notes. She carefully records the date and type of activity. Today, she's watching Aimee during dramatic play.

Observational notes, or anecdotal records, capture each child's cognitive, language, social-emotional, and physical development. They are the foundation for documenting young children's progress, providing a rich, in-depth description of what a teacher observes. Perhaps a teacher wants to measure a child's understanding of a mathematics skill. She can play a game, ask questions, and write down the child's answers or describe how the child explains his or her thinking.

Observational notes are an authentic assessment because they capture a range of skills over time. They capture what children say and do. They show what children know and understand in a detailed and accurate way. Observation notes record emerging strengths along with areas in which a child needs support.

You may think you will remember an event, but without written notes, you won't have a detailed memory. If you are required to record children's progress using a specific curriculum or system, written records ensure you give an accurate and fair rating for each child. The next time you use a required assessment system or prepare for a conference with families, you'll have a collection of specific quotes and descriptions that document meaningful learning.

The chart in Figure 5.2 illustrates how to take notes in a variety of contexts during the day. The headings give you the skill area. The bottom section, "Learning Extensions," is a place to add notes for follow up support, teaching strategies, adaptations and modifications, or extensions for the specific child. You may fill in the chart during one observation or add notes over several days or longer. The goal is to foster the habit of documenting multiple areas of skill development.

Observation Notes Chart

Name: Aimee Smith	**Date:** October 20, 10–10:05 am

Context of observation: Five minutes during dramatic play. Theme of veterinarian care.

Present: JK, DB, and SM

Social-Emotional

Cooperated with JK's plan, even though she was busy with organizing the work tools.
She said, "I am sorry your puppy hurt his foot. Here is a bandage to fix his leg."

Executive Function

Aimee prefers personal space when she plays. Today, she successfully managed
the animal hospital area without distraction or frustration.

Fine and Gross Motor

Aimee removed a complicated bandage from DB's stuffed animal.
She rolled it carefully and put it into the veterinarian kit.

Language and Communication

Aimee used three vocabulary words: *recover*, *exam*, and *allergic*.
She said, "Bruiser's face is red. He is allergic to the food."

Cognitive and Dispositional

Social Studies — The children learned that community services are exchanged for money.

Math — Aimee charged JK $10 for taking care of his pet. She charged $5
for medicine for SM's chicken. She counted individual dollars for each.

Concepts — She said, "It's not expensive." She reminded, "Bring her back again in two weeks."
Aimee asked, "How do veterinarians take care of horses if their offices are too little?"

Learning Extensions

The following books were read and discussed with Aimee:

> *A Day in the Life of a Veterinarian*, by Heather Adamson

> *Biscuit Visits the Doctor,* by Alyssa Satin Capucilli

> *I Want to Be a Veterinarian*, by Laura Driscoll

Figure 5.2. Observation Notes Chart. Illustrates how to take notes in a variety of contexts during the day.

Documenting Progress with Developmental Checklists

> Ms. Keisha sits across a low table from Juan and Aimee. They sort shells to create different number combinations. Ms. Keisha places three shells in a row and taps each one lightly. She counts, "One, two, three. Let's add four more." She points to the third shell and the children count with her as she taps the shells in the line. "Three, four, five, six, seven. Seven shells." Then she asks, "How did we get to seven? We counted up from three."
>
> Ms. Keisha slides shells toward Aimee. "Here are four shells. Can you add two more?" Aimee points and counts, "One, two, three, four." She pauses to move two shells over. She taps the fourth shell and adds on, "Four, five, six."

Ms. Keisha gives the children a way to show what they know. She uses a counting activity with shells to evaluate their understanding of cardinality--knowing that the last word spoken when counting represents the total number of objects in a set. Ms. Keisha uses a checklist to track the children's skills.

Checklists, such as the sample for Aimee in Figure 5.3, keep a record of specific areas of development. The benefit of using a checklist is the ability to zoom in on a sequence of skills. You can add clarifying notes to describe how a skill was observed. You can also track progress in specific content areas, such as math, phonemic awareness, or physical and social skills. This record can then be used to plan additional activities that build emerging skills.

Building a Portfolio Over Time

> Ms. Rachel asks the children what they want to compare. "Shoes," says Quentin. "What kind of shoes?" asks Ms. Rachel. The children decide on shoes that tie, shoes that slip on, and shoes that use Velcro. Ms. Rachel draws vertical and horizontal lines to make a large pictograph.
>
> The children tell Ms. Rachel what kind of shoes they are wearing. She draws one shoe in each square, one above the other. The children count together as Ms. Rachel points: "One, two, three, four. Four shoes tie."
>
> Ms. Rachel asks, "What kind of shoe has more than four?" Quentin answers, "Velcro." Ms. Rachel encourages him to count. "How many Velcro shoes are there?" Quentin starts at the bottom and counts up to five." "Yes," says Ms. Rachel, "five Velcro shoes. Five Velcro shoes are more than four tie shoes."

Next, Ms. Rachel asks the children to choose other data they want to collect. They decide to record the number of their sisters and brothers, what kinds of pets they have, and what they ate for dinner. At the end of the week, when the charts are finished, Ms. Rachel asks each child to explain the concepts of more or less for the items they graphed.

The math objectives for the activity are that children understand that numbers represent objects and pictographs represent information. The objectives for social skills are for children to work together and cooperate to create the graphs. Ms. Rachel will display the pictographs in the classroom to show families. She places a summary record in the children's portfolio. Quentin's summary record is shown in Figure 5.4.

A portfolio compiles work samples for children that are saved over time. It may include original copies of children's work or digital photos of their work that represent time samples throughout a school year. Written notes or summary records, like the one shown in Figure 5.4, describe what children said or did. Consider adding children's dictations, artwork, or writing. You can include science drawings, math representations, and stories. Checklists and other notes and charts that show children's learning and progress are also useful. In this way, a portfolio provides a balanced and complete picture of children's learning.

Sample Checklist for Aimee

Name: Aimee Smith	
Goal	**Date Observed and Notes**
✓ Counts verbally forward and backward to 10	09–20: First in group, then individually
✓ Counts to 20	10–5: Pointed and counted meaningfully to 20 using counting bears
✓ Uses fingers and objects to represent numbers	10–21: Decided how many napkins were needed to set the table
✓ Counts out loud from 1 to 10 pointing to objects (one-to-one correspondence)	10–5: Pointed to printed animals and counted meaningfully while pointing
✓ Recognizes that a group of items represent a certain quantity without counting (subitizing)	11–15: Matched domino numbers (dots) through 8 without counting
✓ Describes the attributes of shapes (square, triangle, circle, rectangle)	11–18: Sorted by three attributes (size, shape, color) and described the number of sides
✓ Knows the last word spoken during counting represents the objects in a set as a whole (cardinality)	12–09: Used understanding of cardinality to add on to objects in a set, adding numbers up to 10
☐ Sorts two types of items by attribute (similar and different)	
☐ Identifies more and less of a quantity	
☐ Uses contrasting concept words *taller/shorter, bigger/smaller, more/less,* and *heavier/lighter*	
☐ Identifies groups of numbers in sets	
☐ Separates and combines groups into sets	
☐ Creates and repeats simple patterns	

Figure 5.3. Sample checklist for Aimee. Demonstrates how to keep a record of development in specific math concepts.

Quentin's Summary Record

Name: Quentin B. Date: 02-17	
Theme/Topic	**Demonstration of Learning for Data Collection**
Shoes	"Five shoes are Velcro. Five is the most. Four are tie shoes. Two shoes slip on."
Pets	"Mary has the most pets. She has two dogs, a cat, and parakeet. George and Nathen have no pets."
Siblings	"Joshua has the most siblings. He has seven brothers and sisters."
Dinner	"Most kids ate macaroni and cheese. Eight people ate macaroni and cheese."
Objectives Children will 1. Understand that numbers represent objects 2. Use graphs to represent information 3. Demonstrate cooperation to complete graphs	**Notes** Quentin represented numbers of items on the graphs with pictures. He pointed to the line and showed his understanding of more or less for numbers up to 10. Quentin worked successfully with Lauren and Michael to document numbers of pets belonging to our class.

Figure 5.4. Quentin's Summary Record. Indicates what Quentin does and says to demonstrate learning.

A graphic organizer or a graph to collect or sort information can provide a useful picture of children's thinking and ideas. Samples of self-portraits and printed names can show progress made in representation over time. Worksheets that require children to fill in replicated items, provide a correct answer, or match pictures to words are not appropriate learning activities for young children. These should not be included in portfolios. Children learn best when interacting with real-life materials, hands-on experiences, and meaningful conversations with peers and teachers. Worksheets offer only closed-ended or repetitive practice, whereas solving real-life problems and collaborative demonstrations allow for deeper levels of conversation and more complex learning.

Taking Photographs and Digital Recordings

Tyler, Kara, and Stephanie wear explorer hats. Kara says, "We are going to the zoo." They hold plastic bins with stuffed animals. Tyler makes a sign that says *zoo* in big red letters. She copies the letters and tapes the paper to the wall over their table.

Mr. Theo asks, "Are you zookeepers? What is your animal and what will it eat?" Tyler says, "I have a porpoise. She eats fish." Kara says, "Grrrrrr. This is my lion. She eats meat." Stephanie says, "My giraffe eats trees." Mr. Theo asks, "Does your giraffe stretch his neck up high to reach the leaves?" Stephanie answers, "My giraffe eats leaves from the acacia tree."

Mr. Theo read *There Was a Tree*, by Rachel Isadora, just before the children's playtime. He sees that Stephanie remembers the acacia tree from the book's version of the song, "The Green Grass Grew All Around."

The girls enjoy acting out books from the science center. They look for a long time at the detailed photographs of animals in *I Want to Be a Zookeeper*, by Dee Phillips. They especially like *Z is for Zookeeper: A Zoo Alphabet*, by Marie and Roland Smith, with its many illustrations that show a zookeeper's jobs.

As the girls are playing, Mr. Theo takes a photo and prints three copies. On the back, he writes what the girls say about their animals. The photo shows Tyler leaning on a mop with rags hanging over her arm. The girls have buckets to carry the animals' food. Stephanie is holding her giraffe up in the air.

Photographs and video recordings capture the details of children's learning moments and dramatic play scenarios. They can document children's work, from three-dimensional artwork to block structures to completed puzzles. Videos may preserve book reenactments, storytelling, children's explanations about their artwork, and math thinking. Group or solitary play, projects and presentations, and poetry or other performance moments can be captured by video. These records can be stored in a digital

portfolio. Photos and videos also provide feedback to children and to families. Children enjoy seeing their work and looking at themselves.

The photo or video documentation gives you new opportunities to talk with children about their learning. During that conversation, you'll learn more about how they think, feel, and make sense of the content they are learning. In addition, writing down or recording what children say when viewing themselves establishes evidence of their understanding. When maintaining a digital portfolio, label each file with the date, title, and child's name. Also record the purpose of the activity and what children were learning. A written record can accompany the digital recordings with standards, objectives, and notes or a checklist to describe the skills children demonstrated in the photo or video.

Preparing Projects and Presentations

> Matilda holds up a small book to show her classmates. She turns the pages slowly as she talks. The drawings are colorful with captions she wrote. She says, "My grandfather is from Portugal. When he was six, he picked grapes and tomatoes. He went to a little school with other children. His favorite memory is making ice cream. They put salt in a bucket and turned the handle. Avô says it is the most delicious ever."

Ms. Celena works with the local librarian to select books that reflect the children's families. She reads *Who's in My Family? All About Our Families*, by Robie H. Harris, and *My Family, Your Family*, by Lisa Bullard, to the children. She secures brown paper to the large side wall. Over several weeks, the children paint portraits of their families. Ms. Celena attaches these to the mural with captions.

The children interview a family member. They ask, "What chores did you do when you were my age?," "What was it like to go to school?," and "What is your favorite childhood memory?" The children create a book with pictures they draw. Ms. Celena helps them write the answers to the questions. The books will be holiday presents for the children's families.

The mural project and family books incorporate many skills. The learning objectives include understanding that families are the same and different. Through the family questions, children learn that people grow and change over time. Creative expression is needed for drawing and painting. The children listen and retell stories that have a beginning, a middle, and an end. These are important social studies, language, and communication goals for the preschool year.

Projects are tangible and give children a chance to take pride in what they do. Projects can include culminating activities like presentations, picture journals, and two- or three-dimensional products created by children. Documentation boards or murals can display children's work and dictation. They get to share their ideas and learn from each other.

When planning projects, be realistic about the time necessary to plan and obtain the material. You'll need to know your children well to ensure they have the skills and support needed. This is a great time to work with families, volunteers, and support staff, such as a librarian to facilitate ideas and activities. Figure 5.5 demonstrates how Ms. Celena documents the children's work using photos, a checklist, and written notes.

Matilda's Photos, Checklist, and Notes

Name: Matilda C.   **Date:** 04-21

Title: Family Interview and Book

Objectives: Children will

- ✓ Understand that families are the same and different

- ✓ Understand that people and circumstances change over time

- ✓ Demonstrate creative expression in drawing and painting

- ✓ Communicate using complete sentences

- ✓ Retell story with beginning, middle, and end

- ✓ Depict story reflecting a true story

- ✓ Listen to the ideas and experiences of others

Notes

*See attached photographs of book illustrations and mural painting.

Matilda talked with her grandfather. She shared his experience in Portugal at the age of 6, helping in the garden and making ice cream.

Field Note: Inviting Families to Celebrate Learning

We invited families to our Growing Great Gardens project presentation. The children created egg cartons with seedlings, sprouts growing in plastic containers, and cups with lettuce and kale. They made posters with drawings of their plants. Our class project included a window box that was not at all perfect. But everything in it was edible. The children helped me label everything in Spanish and English. When the families came, children shared one important fact and one "how-to" skill from their growing project. We sent home indoor gardening tips and the children left with their plants and drawings. It was worth the dirt on the floor, the planning, and the effort. The videos and photos were amazing. I was so proud of the children and so were their families.

Figure 5.5. Matilda's Photos, Checklist, and Notes. Demonstrates how to document children's work using photos, a checklist, and written notes.

Evaluating Progress with Emerging, Demonstrating, Exceeding Descriptors

> Molly holds her box tightly and says, "She's like Hedgie in *Hedgie's Surprise.* That's why I like her. I like Hedgie. Hedgehogs make grunting sounds. That's why they sound like a hog." Molly makes grunting sounds, and the children giggle. Molly continues. "They hibernate. That means they sleep all winter. They are spiky, but the pokes don't hurt their family."
>
> Ms. Veronica asks, "Does anyone have questions?" Liza asks, "What is in your box?" Molly says, "It's leaves. I have leaves so Hedgie can sleep." George says, "My friend has a pet hedgehog. He sleeps in a cage."

To get the children started on a habitat project, Ms. Veronica reads *Don't Wake Up the Bear!* by Marjorie Dennis Murray. It is one of many books (see Figure 5.6) that the children explore together as they make habitat boxes where animals can hibernate. They work around a large table with bits of leaves, grass, moss, and sticks. They dip paintbrushes into brown, black, and white tempera paint mixed thickly so it will stick to the shoe boxes.

In addition to reading the books, the children cut pictures from *Ranger Rick* and *National Geographic Kids* magazines. They choose chipmunks, bears, bats, snakes, hedgehogs, and skunks. Ms. Veronica plays video clips and shows slides of the animals on the *National Geographic Kids* website.

Ms. Veronica and Ms. Khadijah create a cave area in the classroom. There is an assortment of stuffed animals, along with sticks, empty boxes, and blankets. The children pretend to be animals in the winter.

During the week, Ms. Veronica also turns the children's attention to animal coverings, such as fur and feathers, that keep animals and birds warm. Together, they make a map of the "forest" (their classroom). The children stick laminated animal tracks to the floor. There is a key chart that identifies the names of the animals with drawings of the tracks. They have great fun finding the tracks in the classroom using the chart.

Ms. Veronica needs to document what the children have learned. Detailed written and descriptive feedback fits the needs of these young children. She decides to use a rating scale to show skills that are emerging, independent, or exceeding the objectives.

Rating scales use specific criteria from early learning guidelines or developmental milestones. A strengths-based system documents children's increasing competence. Describing increasing levels of competence, as done in the following examples, can help do this:

Emerging. As you support children's learning, you might need to give a cue or prompt for a child to remember the name of a body part or to describe an animal. You may need to give some physical assistance to complete a task. These skills can be said to be *beginning* or *emerging with support*. Over time, children can demonstrate skills with increasing independence. They may need only minor prompting to explain their thinking.

Independent. Eventually, children can demonstrate skills independently. For example, they may be able to choose an animal and carry out the steps in creating a habitat without support. These skills can be described as *meeting* a goal or as an *independent* skill.

Exceeding. Finally, some children may demonstrate skills in language, physical dexterity, or cognitive development that are beyond the learning objective. They may explore information about additional animals, talk about the body's response to cold, or discuss an animal's safety. These skills can be described as *exceeding*.

The goal is to use words that capture what children *can* do instead of what they can't. You can define each level to fit with your program, school, district, or state recommendations. Whatever system you use, strengths-based descriptions allow you and families to understand and talk about where children are in the natural progression of their learning and development. The sample emergent skill chart featured in Figure 5.6 includes a four-part scale: beginning, approaching, meeting, and exceeding.

Molly's Emergent Skill Chart

	Child's Name: Molly B.	**Date:** 03–17	
Topic: Animals in Winter — Habitat Project			

	Objective 1 Science: Collect, describe, and compare information about animals in winter.	**Objective 2** Language: Use new words learned through conversation and reading (*migrate, hibernate, adapt*).	**Objective 3** Art: Create a three-dimensional representation to show a concept or idea.
Exceeding: Goes beyond stated objective to add additional information or demonstrates understanding of more complex ideas		*Molly used the words *migrate, hibernate,* and *adapt* and supported her ideas. During the presentation, she explained that hedgehogs sleep through the winter.	
Meeting: Independently meets objective and demonstrates understanding of content without assistance.	*Molly sorted animals in matching game to those that migrate, hibernate, and are awake during the winter.		*Molly created a winter habitat for a hedgehog independently. See attached photo.
Approaching: Meets the objective and understands content with minor or minimal support.			
Beginning: Meets the objective with assistance.			

Notes: Molly demonstrated independence in carrying out steps for her project. She supported her peers' work and listened well.

Book Topic: Migration and Hibernation

> *Animals in Winter,* by Henrietta Bancroft
> *Birds in Winter,* by Jenny Fretland VanVoorst
> *Don't Wake Up the Bear!* by Marjorie Dennis Murray
> *Goose's Story,* by Cari Best
> *Hibernation,* by Margaret Hall

> *Over and Under the Snow,* by Kate Messner
> *Sleep Big Bear, Sleep,* by Maureen Wright
> *What Animals Do in Winter,* by Melvin Berger
> *When Winter Comes,* by Pearl Neuman

Figure 5.6. Sample emergent skill chart. This four-part scale uses specific criteria from early learning guidelines or developmental milestones to document children's increasing competence.

Using Commercial Assessments

Ms. Lisa hugs the children goodbye and makes tea. She sits quietly at her desk and opens her computer. For the next few minutes, she reviews Jessica's portfolio and the notes she has written about letter recognition and letter-sound knowledge. She wants to be sure she has in mind exactly what skills Jessica has demonstrated. She opens the webpage for the assessment scale required by her program. She uses a portfolio checklist to record Jessica's skills in the system.

Next, Ms. Lisa views the digital video of Jessica and Daria as they retell *Zinnia's Flower Garden*, by Monica Wellington. She laughs when she hears Jessica say, "This gardening is dirty business." She is certain Jessica has heard that phrase from a family member. Returning to the checklist, she marks *yes*, Jessica can retell familiar stories in sequence using details about the characters, events, and storylines.

Commercial assessments can provide an accurate picture of development over time. Your program may participate in collecting data using products such as the Ages and Stages Questionnaires (ASQ), the Kent Inventory of Developmental Skills (KIDS), or the Early Development Index (EDI). Perhaps you use the HighScope Curriculum and related Child Observation Record. Many programs use Teaching Strategies GOLD, which evaluates progress in children's development. Other programs use the Work Sampling System to compile data. Play-based programs may use the Penn Interactive Peer Play Scale (PIPPS) to evaluate social skills during play. Specific tools focus on a defined number of skills or may capture a global picture of children's development across a range of skills.

Validity and reliability ensure that an assessment tool shows an accurate picture of specific skills for the specific children and context. *Valid* means the instrument

> Accurately measures the stated skills and abilities

> Has been reviewed for appropriateness for the age of children and situation

> Is developmentally, culturally, and linguistically appropriate, as well as appropriate for children with disabilities

Reliable means the instrument

> Accurately represents the skills and abilities of the children

> Provides a consistent picture of children's skills whether used at one time or another

> Provides results consistent across groups of children and is comparable across settings and contexts

For commercial assessment use, training is essential to ensure fidelity to the purpose and processes of documentation. *Fidelity* means that whether you use the tool or another teacher uses it, you both do it in the same way. The results should be the same for a child, no matter who gives the assessment. You must know how to use the tool and be aware of factors that can influence outcomes.

Assessment tools are used in *authentic contexts*—that is, typical experiences—and administered or completed by adults who know the children well. When there are cultural or linguistic differences, every effort should be made to secure someone who speaks the same language as the child and with whom the child feels comfortable. Evaluation should ensure

Consistency over time. No matter what kind of assessment approach is used, no one moment in time or one type of evaluation should be used to represent what a child can do. Appropriate assessment uses different ways of observing children during different times of day and across weeks.

Identification of specific skills. You must be able to identify distinct skills, as well as understand how skills impact other competencies. For example, to evaluate a child's behavior, you must recognize whether a situation is related to verbal or physical skills.

The context of development. Development can come in spurts, as some areas leap ahead of others. In addition, daily patterns of competence are impacted by fatigue, lack of exercise, nutritional needs, and stress.

Children are sensitive to inconsistency and changes in the setting. Evaluation must always take into consideration the context.

Use of objective data. You'll need to be sure that the ratings you give children are anchored by specific documentation. This ensures ratings are determined from facts rather than from perceptions.

Evaluating with a purpose. The purpose of assessment is to provide information you need to teach effectively. Your goal is to use what you learn to build children's competence and to provide support for their development and learning. What have you discovered about the child's strengths and emerging skills that will guide your teaching?

Assessing and Supporting Children Who Are Linguistically Diverse

Ms. Aisha sits quietly with Jieun and Hwan. Together, they complete a number matching game. There are large dots on one set of cards with images of animals and children on the other. Ms. Aisha writes notes while she is with the children but stays focused on them.

"How many cats? *Goyang-i myeoch maliya?*" Ms. Aisha reads the question she has written in Korean. The boys answer together, "Eight cats. *Goyang-i yeodeolb mali.*"

Ms. Asisha gives them each a high-five. She points to the dots and counts to eight. She points to the cats and counts to eight. She helps the boys point and count. She asks, "What is this?" The boys tell her that a dog is *gae*, a boy is *soneon*, and a fish is *milgogi*. They count the numbers by pointing to the dots and the pictures.

Ms. Asisha documents the numbers the boys accurately point and count. She makes a note to look up the Korean words for *dog, boy,* and *fish* so she can spell them correctly. She communicates with sounds and gestures, barking for the dog and wiggling her hand for the fish. Her language isn't perfect, but the math is accomplished, and they have fun. The boys are unaware that they have been assessed.

Assessments that are a natural part of daily play experiences help children focus on the task without anxiety or fear. The positive relationship Jieun and Hwan share with Ms. Aisha keeps their brains focused and their bodies relaxed. They look forward to playing more games with her.

When you work with multilingual learners, it is important to understand the factors that impact assessment (Kim et al. 2018). Some teachers hold misperceptions about the level of support children need (Jacoby & Lesaux 2019). With multilingual children, it is important to

> Learn about the differences in dual language learners' language acquisition sequence and timing.

> Use assessments that don't rely exclusively on English skill and verbal communication.

> Recognize that children's performance is impacted by time of day, activity, circumstances, and well-being.

> Explore the many differences among dual-language or multi-lingual learners backgrounds. There is tremendous diversity within, between, and among linguistic groups.

> Reflect on the ways linguistic and cultural differences can influence perceptions about children's capability or progress. Judgments can be formed inaccurately by taking only speaking skills into consideration.

> Consider the ways cultural differences influence children's ways of communicating with a teacher. Some children may look down or not maintain eye contact. Prior learning may have required listening to a teacher quietly rather than expecting children to respond or interact.

What can you do to assess multilingual learners' progress accurately? Sensitivity is needed to develop a trusting relationship that helps children feel safe expressing themselves in new ways. Give many opportunities for children to show what they know and can do. Be sure you check for learning using performance assessments where children can demonstrate their skills without relying only on language for communication. Observe children in a variety of situations. Support children as they think about and process information. Provide positive and encouraging learning experiences. Over time, you'll gain a comprehensive picture of their developing strengths and skills.

Figure 5.7. Example of a child-created alphabet. (Reprinted from Alanís, I., Arreguín M., & Salinas González, I. 2021. *The Essentials: Supporting Dual Language Learners in Diverse Environments in Preschool and Kindergarten.* Washington, DC: NAEYC.)

To strengthen children's understanding

> Include informational texts, pictures, and stories that relate to daily experiences of the children.

> Pre-teach and model academic language and vocabulary using real-life modeling, objects, and examples.

> Introduce concepts in multiple ways using stories and events from children's lives.

Work with children to support their skills through shared games, activities, and conversation. Child-created alphabets empower dual language learners to think about familiar words and images that emerge from their family, community, or classroom experiences. For example, after a class discussion about what makes families unique, each child is given a paper with a letter of the alphabet and a blank space for them to write words or create

illustrations that describe what makes their family unique, such as *B* for *bilingual, C* for *cook, L* for *loving,* and so on. Children's direct participation contributes to their understanding of individual phonemes in words they have experienced and that have meaning to them and their families (Alanís, Arreguín, & Salinas-González, 2021).

Keep checking on children's understanding to see if there is anything else you can introduce, modify, or provide that will support or clarify learning.

BALANCE POINTS

Seeing from the Child's Point of View

During daily events, consider interactions from the children's point of view. What messages did they hear you say about their way of doing things, their capabilities, and their efforts? How did an experience feel to them? The preschool year can leave an indelible impression on children's perceptions of themselves as learners. Words and messages can have lasting impact. It helps to "stand in their shoes" to consider what they most need.

Each child is unique. Some children develop skills that emerge in an expected sequence. Some children show asynchronous development, with certain skills leaping ahead and others lagging behind. Sleep, rest, atypical routines, and changes in the family schedule can impact the way children function. Stress and fluctuations in children's health and well-being impact children's development from day to day and over time. For these reasons, developmental progress is always evaluated in context, taking into consideration all factors that influence children's experiences over time.

READY RESOURCES

Building on Developmental Milestones

Developmental milestones are presented by the Centers for Disease Control and Prevention (CDC) to provide common language for families to use with pediatricians and others involved in the care and education of children. The CDC "Know the Signs: Act

Early" initiative promotes universal early screening for all young children. The goal is to promote healthy development and to encourage early identification for children with disabilities at a time when intervention can be most effective (Weitzman 2019).

The evaluation of children's progress needs to be framed in a holistic perspective, with responsiveness to and understanding of a wide range of diversities. Children's experiences vary due to cultural contexts, experiences, and individual differences. Screenings must be scrutinized carefully to ensure appropriateness for the context of each specific child. There must be no linguistic or cultural bias in screening content or processes. Families, cultural brokers, and diverse professionals should be included in screening processes to ensure a fair and accurate picture. Those who participate must "fully consider the specific abilities, interests, experiences, and motivations of a particular child or their family's culture, preferences, values, and child-rearing practices when determining the most appropriate practice for that child" (NAEYC 2020, 34).

The following resources present developmental milestones and include additional information to help you apply understanding of child development to your teaching practices. Included are milestones from birth to age 3 so that you can evaluate preschool children's progress in context.

> American Academy of Pediatrics Developmental Milestones: www.aap.org/sites/Search/Pages/results.aspx?k=developmental+milestone

> Centers for Disease Control and Prevention (CDC) Developmental Milestones, Checklists, and Screening Tools: www.cdc.gov/ncbddd/actearly/milestones/index.html

> CDC Milestones in Action Video Library: www.cdc.gov/ncbddd/actearly/milestones/milestones-in-action.html

> CDC *Watch Me! Celebrating Milestones and Sharing Concerns*: www.cdc.gov/ncbddd/watchmetraining/index.html

> National Association for Gifted Children: www.nagc.org/resources-publications/resources-parents/young-bright-children

> National Institute on Deafness and Other Communication Disorders Speech and Language Developmental Milestones and Checklists: www.nidcd.nih.gov/health/speech-and-language

> Pathways Child Growth and Development Resources: https://pathways.org/use-books-boost-vocabulary-communication-skills

> WIDA Resources for Educators and Practitioners: https://wida.wisc.edu/memberships/early-years

> Zero to Three Child Development Age-Based Tips Birth to 36 Months for Families: www.zerotothree.org/resources/series/your-child-s-development-age-based-tips-from-birth-to-36-months

While milestones of development provide a broad framework for child development, it is important to keep in mind that each area of development is interdependent with others. For example, verbal skills impact social development. Fine motor coordination may influence when and how children demonstrate other skills. Importantly, cultural priorities and values influence the timing and development of skills, learning, and behavior. All children develop in unique ways and at different times.

As you plan your setting, materials, and activities, the most important priority is to know individual children well. Use carefully planned observation to gain a complete picture of children's strengths and needs. With that information, lesson plans will meet the needs of the whole group, while also addressing developmental needs for each child.

READY RESOURCES

Understanding Early Screening and Intervention

The American Academy of Pediatrics recommends that all children be screened for general development using standardized, validated tools at 9, 18, and 24 or 30 months and for autism at 18 and 24 months, or whenever a family or provider has a concern. Screenings are used with the family's permission to identify variations in development, including behavior, physical skill, language and cognitive development, and emotional and social skills. Collaborating with families and community resources can ensure the best possible outcomes for every child.

When children speak a language other than English, a teacher who speaks the same home language must conduct the screening. This person must know and understand the child's language and culture and have sufficient skill level in the child's home language to accurately administer the screening. Because they share the same language and culture, this professional will understand the context of the child's responses, interactions, and communications.

When children require additional services or support, families can be referred to a local agency that will conduct a more formal evaluation to determine eligibility for early intervention services. Section 504 of the Rehabilitation Act ensures that children with disabilities are not excluded from programs on the basis of a disability. Services and supports may be available through a child's health insurance, or it may be required for a program to provide services and supports through Section 504 of the Rehabilitation Act, if the child is qualified. The Individuals with Disabilities Education Act (IDEA) requires programs to follow specific guidelines for screening.

For children with disabilities, teachers must use instructional practices to meet individual goals. You will use your understanding of developmental milestones and individual development as you design, arrange, equip, and adapt spaces to teach children of varying ages and abilities. The environment, materials, and teaching strategies must ensure full access and participation for all children.

The following resources from the CDC offer additional information about screening for young children:

> Developmental Monitoring and Screening: www. cdc.gov/ncbddd/childdevelopment/screening.html

> Compendium of Screening Measures for Young Children: www.acf.hhs.gov/sites/default/files/ecd/screening_compendium_march2014.pdf

HELPFUL HINT

Sharing Assessment Information with Families

As you have seen, authentic samples of children's work are those that are collected during typical activities of the classroom. These include anecdotal records—written notes about what children say and do and notes written during observations—as well as other kinds of documentation, such as photographs, quotes, samples of work, and video clips. These are resources to share with families.

A narrative summary should be included that describes children's progress. Your statements should be strengths-based and focus on emerging skills. Some programs and school districts require portfolio information shared with families to have specific state benchmarks or developmental checklists included. These show how children are progressing in the expected content for the pre-K year.

Committing to Ethical Practice

Ethical practice is essential as you observe, document, and assess children's progress. There are multiple ways to adhere to ethical standards in assessment, screening practices, record keeping, and communication. You will need to keep up to date on the most current information regarding research-based assessment practices, as these must protect children from bias and inaccurate conclusions.

Ensuring Objectivity

All assessment approaches described in this chapter require a stringent level of oversight to ensure that evaluations of children are fair and accurate. Teachers need to think about favoritism and emotional contexts to be sure all children are evaluated objectively. For example, they may rate a child with behavior challenges more harshly in the cognitive domain than a child with whom they do not struggle. They also must ensure that evaluation honors linguistic and cultural differences. The goal isn't to judge a child's progress, but to look for ways to use the results of an observation or evaluation to guide teaching practices and to shift and adapt the level and kind of support to encourage increasing development.

Protecting Privacy

Ethical practice also requires maintaining the highest level of privacy and confidentiality. For example, teachers must put away assessment materials and notes when families or others are in the classroom. They must share information with families at appropriate times when children are not present to pick up or internalize confusing messages. Teachers should not discuss children's progress in front of other families and children. Children's progress should be discussed with the program director and specialists only when the time and place is private and conversations cannot be overheard.

Using a Strengths-Based Lens

Ethical practice requires commitment to strengths-based communication. When information is shared with families, it should be presented from a strengths-based perspective, using language that focuses on beginning, emerging, and strengthening skills rather than on deficits or weaknesses. When talking with families, communicate in factual and supportive ways.

When a child's progress raises a concern, teachers should communicate positive expectations. For example, "We would like to see your child supported in the area of book reading to help develop his interest and skills," rather than "We notice your child does not like to read books." Or "We can work together on this skill and have confidence your child can do this," rather than "Your child's behavior is interrupting lunch." Words convey powerful messages. Using strengths-based communication is essential.

Choosing an Appropriate Means of Communication

Ethical practice requires choosing the appropriate means of communication. For example, children's personal or assessment information should not be communicated by teachers to families in emails, over text, or by phone. Discussions about children's development should always take place between the teacher and families in-person and not in front of any another person or child. Individual meetings can be set up by email, text, or phone. More information about communication will be covered in Chapter 6.

Protecting Data

Ethical practice requires protection of data. This means using stringent passwords for all digital files and locking file drawers that contain personal or identifiable information about children and families. It means shredding all discarded papers that have personally identifiable information or written notes that describe a specific child or children. Password protection is also required for apps and social media pages where documentation of children (e.g., photographs, videos, written descriptions) is present. All practices and guidelines must be considered as they relate to your unique program to ensure the highest level of privacy and confidentiality.

Applying Professional Guidelines

The NAEYC Code of Ethical Conduct and Statement of Commitment (2011, 2) presents important information to support your professional practice. It states that you will "base program practices on current knowledge and research in the field of early childhood education, child development, and related disciplines, as well as on particular knowledge of each child" (I–1.2). In the context of assessment, you will "recognize and respect the unique qualities, abilities, and potential of each child" (I–1.3). You will "appreciate the vulnerability of children and their dependence on adults" (I–1.4). You will "use assessment instruments and strategies that are appropriate for the children to be assessed, that are used only for the purposes for which they were designed, and that have the potential to benefit children" (I–1.6). Finally, you will "use assessment information to understand and support children's development and learning, to support instruction, and to identify children who may need additional services" (I–1.7).

NAEYC Standard 4 addresses assessment of child progress. It ensures that programs use a variety of formal and informal approaches to provide information on children's learning and development. The purpose of assessment is to inform decisions about the children, to improve teaching practices, and to drive program improvement.

The NAEYC standards ensure that assessment occurs "in the context of reciprocal communications between teachers and families, with sensitivity to the cultural contexts in which children are developing" (2018, 53). Professionals must

> Use appropriate assessment methods (4.B)

> Use developmental assessment and screening to identify children's interests, needs, and to describe progress (4.C)

> Adapt curriculum and individualize teaching (4.D)

> Communicate with and involve families in the assessment process (4.E)

> Use assessment data during collaborative planning times talk with colleagues about how to support children's development and learning (4D.4)

> Continue to adjust teaching strategies based on information gained from child assessment outcomes (4D.6)

REFLECTION QUESTIONS

1. What forms of child assessment do you use most often? Which developmental and learning skills do these assessments capture?

2. Which authentic assessment approaches would you like to incorporate more effectively in your teaching practice? How would these changes more accurately measure children's progress over time?

3. What specific benefits will authentic assessments provide for children from differing cultures and linguistic backgrounds?

4. How can more effective observation, documentation, and assessment practices improve your lesson planning and teaching?

5. Even while maintaining ethical and privacy regulations about the details of specific children's needs and records, conversations with colleagues can provide insights about the best approaches to observation, documentation, assessment, and portfolio processes. How can reflective communication with colleagues help you improve your practices to better meet the needs of children?

CHAPTER 6

Enriching Communication with Families and Colleagues

Planning and Communication as Anchors of High Quality

Maria straightens her classroom quickly. She tosses a floppy bunny into a large woven basket with the stuffed animals and wipes the table. She sets a file folder and her laptop on the table.

Mr. Munoz, Tricia's father, knocks at the door. "Hi, Ms. Maria. How are you?" Maria smiles. "Hello, Mr. Munoz. I can't wait to talk with you about Tricia. She's growing leaps and bounds. She wrote and illustrated a story for you. Come join me, and I'll show you."

Maria worked for several months to organize her portfolio system, with systematic notes and photos to document children's progress. She helped the children complete several projects, including illustrated stories, a mural display with children's paintings depicting families, and digital videos to capture children's dramatic play. These are ready to share at family conferences. The knowledge she gains from families helps her design an inclusive and relevant classroom.

Family engagement is designed to make interactions positive for everyone. But there is a great deal of work involved and a lot at stake. In order for communication to be effective, it needs to be anchored in your deep knowledge of each child, your ability to understand families' perspectives, and well-organized planning. Lesson planning is dependent on reciprocal communication with families. Your effectiveness is influenced by the attitudes, knowledge, and behaviors that affect communication and trust (OPRE 2011). *Attitudes* include perceptions about families and evaluation of contexts that impact their well-being. *Knowledge* includes understanding of family cultures, values, and linguistic contexts, as well as your own. *Behaviors* include reflection about the way you come across and the messages communicated to families. As you reflect, you evaluate your impact and recognize the influence of strengths-based language. The knowledge you gain from families will help you design activities for children that reflect and build on the strengths and experiences of their lives.

Communication with families depends on a relationship-based philosophy and genuine collaboration that increases trust. Your knowledge of families will help you connect what you know about their lives to support children's learning. Their knowledge of you is anchored in your commitment and investment in their child's success.

A *relationship-based approach* to family engagement includes a priority on family engagement that is "anchored in intentionally attending to the emotional quality of interactions, with the understanding that parent-child relationships and teacher-child relationships are at the center of children's positive long-term development and learning outcomes" (Virmani, Wiese, & Mangione 2016, 97). School readiness is rooted in the parent-child relationship and each family's cultural and linguistic assets. Communication with families is intentional, collaborative, and coordinated to ensure you learn all you can about the context of children's lives.

A *co-caring model of care* is a relationship-based approach to planning and teaching that builds on communication with families to empower children's success (Julius 2017). It includes authentic communication, mutual support, and coordination of goals (Lang et al. 2016). This approach builds on the resources and assets of families as essential for informed decision making. Children's relationships with their families are the source of their identity and the framework for their learning. You invite families to be partners with you to ensure consistency between the home and your classroom. You learn what is important to the family and understand their priorities for children.

Relationship-based teaching is a priority area set by professional competencies (Schmit & Matthews 2013; Sosinsky et al. 2016). NAEYC Early Learning Program Standard 1 (Relationships) focuses on the foundational need for positive relationships with families as the source of essential knowledge to inform teaching choices. State early development and learning guidelines, along with a rich body of research evidence, demonstrate the need for a secure, safe, and positive setting for learning. Lesson planning must be anchored in shared decision making and goal setting that depends on ongoing, reciprocal communication (NAEYC 2018). This approach builds on children's formative experiences at home and gives you the needed knowledge to plan effective lessons.

RESEARCH CONNECTIONS

Strengthening Teaching with Family Engagement

Relationship-based teaching offers many benefits to children, families, and programs. You rely on families' strengths, competencies, and resources to guide problem-solving and planning as you set positive goals for children (OPRE 2011). In this way, your teaching integrates and builds on families' cultural and linguistic strengths and on the resources and assets of the community.

The following are benefits of relationship-based family engagement:

> Teachers' knowledge and understanding about children and families establishes trust and security among teachers, children, and family members (Owen et al. 2008).

> Teachers' sensitivity and responsiveness to families promote optimal early development (Sosinsky et al. 2016).

> Teachers' strong relationships with families increase the quality of caregiving and communication and result in fewer behavior problems for children (Ruprecht, Elicker, & Choi 2016).

> Family engagement promotes greater security and social-emotional development for children over time (Mortensen & Barnett 2015).

> Family engagement is a protective factor for children from underserved communities with economic insecurity and improves social outcomes and overall academic performance (McWayne, Campos, & Owsianik 2008).

> Family engagement establishes a strong foundation for children's lifelong success and learning in academic and social-emotional development (Fantuzzo et al. 2013; Galindo & Sheldon 2012; Powell et al. 2010).

Family engagement leads to greater achievement, higher grades and test scores, increased enrollment in higher-level programs, stronger graduation rates, and enrollment in post-secondary education (Nguyen, Smith, & Granja 2018).

Sharing Information Using Strengths-Based Language

> Aamir's mother, Cora, comes and goes quietly. She doesn't visit with her child in the classroom or talk with Ms. Dana before leaving. Even though Ms. Dana invites Cora to stay, she leaves quickly.
>
> Ms. Dana talks with her program director. She's worried that Cora's curt departures mean she is dissatisfied or upset. Ms. Mayra encourages Ms. Dana to schedule a meeting to learn more. When they meet, Cora expresses great respect for the program and gratefulness for Aamir's adjustment. She explains that she must catch the train each morning to get to work. Ms. Dana responds by expressing her commitment to Aamir's growth and learning.

Cora's cultural background places a high value of respect and honor for teachers. She shows respect by remaining quiet, while Ms. Dana struggles to interpret that quietness. In order to facilitate communication, flexibility and sensitivity to cultural differences are required.

Different ways of speaking and differing communication styles can act as barriers to open communication (Beneke & Cheatham 2015). Sometimes, issues of power and control or differences in decision-making approaches prohibit successful communication (Hedges & Lee 2010). Interactions with families require sensitivity, willingness to learn, and reflection about the ways people think and relate to others. Interacting with families from a strengths-based perspective is a critical foundation for success.

A *strengths-based approach* embraces the life values, resources, knowledge, and social networks of families. A focus on cultural strengths and funds of knowledge shifts the framework from families as "disadvantaged" to the understanding of people as being fully functioning within a unique cultural setting (Velez-Ibanez 1988; Wolf 1966). An asset-oriented mindset ensures that you keep a strengths-based viewpoint without assuming limitations due to cultural or socioeconomic status. A strengths-based approach shifts from the idea that there is a "right" way of doing things to seeing families as fully competent in raising their children.

Cultural beliefs, attitudes, and values related to families' and caregivers' roles in children's care and education may differ. Some families believe it is their responsibility to be involved in education, whereas others think it is the teacher's or caregiver's sole authority to instruct children (Calzada et al. 2015). Some families feel they can help by teaching proper behaviors at home but do not feel it is their place to participate in the classroom. They may not feel comfortable attending program events (Durand 2011; Maríñez-Lora & Quintana 2009). Some families want the classroom to be teacher directed and structured. They don't feel comfortable when they observe less structured child-centered activities. Ideas about compliance and assertiveness, independence, and collaboration may differ between home and school (Suizzo, Tedford, & McManus 2019; Yang & Li 2019).

For immigrant families or those who are new to an area, many barriers are present, including language. Rather than consider families who speak English as a second language, are from low-income households, or are from other cultures as "at risk," it is important to get to know individual families based on their strengths. Creating a safe and inclusive space for everyone begins with challenging your own assumptions while demonstrating sensitivity to the experiences and perceptions of families. Here are some strategies to get started:

> ❯ Learn all you can about the traditions and practices of the families of the children in your care. Ask children, "What do you like to do at home? How do you do this at home?"

> Include approaches to learning that honor and highlight both the home language and English in materials you share with families. Be sure that you understand language differences so that you can provide appropriate levels of translation, written materials, and other supports.

> Provide books, photos, games, food, dolls, and toys that represent the cultures of all children in your care and of their families. Ask families to share items that they would like to see added, such as books and games.

> When you are not sure about an issue, ask for clarification: "I want so much for your child to be happy here and for you to be satisfied with the care she receives. Is there anything I can do to make this a more positive experience for you?"

> Use positive language to describe children's progress: "Joseph has been counting pegs and toys in the classroom. I'd like for you to help him count when you put things away at home and when he goes to the grocery store with you. Working together will strengthen his math skills." (Rather than saying "Joseph really should be counting to ten by now.")

> Communicate positive expectations: "Travis is showing more interest in reading. He especially likes looking at books about animals. Our librarian has pulled several books that you can read with Travis at home. I know that the more you and I read to him, the more he will look at books independently." (Rather than saying "I am worried that Travis is not showing more interest in reading.")

> Use strengths-based language to talk about and ask questions about families. "I'd like to learn more about" is a great sentence starter. With families, say, "I'd like to learn more about your experiences in Mexico," or "I'd like to know more about the goals you have for your child." With colleagues, say, "I'd like to learn more about how you talk with children's families," or "I'd like to learn more about how you incorporate children's home experiences in your classroom." Inviting others to share their experiences is a great way to gain new perspectives.

> When English is not the home language, set up a sequence of meetings with families and schedule a translator. Be sure materials are available for families in their home language and that the translator encourages the family to ask questions. Establishing regular meetings builds trusts and gives you the needed opportunity to get to know the family and their children better.

> Draw families' attention to children's strengths: "Have you noticed how Erica takes the lead? She's wonderful in helping her friends get organized in a game" and "Today, Meishi put aside her puzzle to help Michael sort his pieces. She was patient and kind as they put the puzzle together." When you highlight children's strengths, families are more likely to notice and support those emerging skills. In this way, you work together to encourage children's competence at school and at home.

By knowing each family well, you can build on the practices that are familiar to the children, including knowledge of the way families dress and eat, how food is prepared, and familiar toys in play. Take time to learn the way families support their children. Learn the songs and stories that are shared at home. Incorporating these into the daily life of the classroom helps children identify with learning and also makes families feel welcome.

Field Note: Building Interest with Questions

In my weekly family connection email, I state our upcoming theme. For example, "This week we are going to focus on nutrition," or "This week, we are going to collect data. The children will learn how to count and represent objects." Families never responded to the emails, and I thought this was normal. Then—without really evaluating the strategy—I added a question and suggested a simple activity: "This week, we are going to study healthy energy balance. We'll be talking about healthy bodies. Does your child know that sometimes the heart beats slowly and sometimes it beats quickly? Ask your child to place a hand over the heart and feel the beat after sitting. Then try jumping up and down. Feel the heart again. What does your child say about the heart beating fast or slow?" Families and children couldn't stop talking about what they had learned. Now I include a question and brief activity each time.

Over time, you and your colleagues will develop a deeper knowledge about extended families and the way family resources strengthen the social skills and experiences of each child. The trust formed between families and you will benefit children's adjustment and growth.

Your program can incorporate aspects of life from families to create a unique culture of shared understanding and practice, where all come to know and appreciate the contributions of home and those of the program (Massing, Kirova, & Henning 2016). Incorporating families' cultures into your teaching helps children value the ideas and practices of others and understand themselves in the context of others. The integrated connections between home and school create a secure space for children to thrive.

Foundations for Integrating Culture

With practical steps, you can infuse your classroom with connections to children's lives at home. You can build on family strengths, cultures, languages, ideas, and experiences. Here's how to learn more:

> Talk with colleagues to develop sensitivity to and knowledge about the cultures and languages represented in your program. Consider new ways to support children's identities and incorporate teaching strategies and supports that represent more than mainstream pedagogy and ideas (Guo 2015).

> Use reflective practice as you engage in authentic dialogue with families and co-construct a mutual understanding of children's needs in the context of their specific identities (Virmani, Wiese, & Mangione 2016).

> Take time to understand the complex needs of children from linguistically diverse families. Learn from and with them to ensure success for children (Czik & Lewis 2016).

> Ask families to tell you about children's play and daily experiences at home. Incorporate their interests, activities, and ways of playing into classroom materials and experiences (Yahya & Wood 2017).

> Keep notes about what families tell you as they pick up and drop off children. Daily communication is rich with stories and experiences children have outside of your classroom. The more you know and remember, the more you can include these ideas in teaching and play.

Evaluate your classroom from the perspective of families. Do any structures or values inadvertently perpetuate an imbalance of opportunity or interfere with children's success (NAEYC, 2020; Wright 2011)? Barriers may be hidden, such as lack of representation by families in leadership roles or lack of family participation in program planning and feedback (Hernandez et al. 2017; Pratt, Lipscomb, & Schmitt 2015). Ensure that families are welcomed as essential partners in children's learning, active participants in decision making, and collaborative advocates for the needs of their children.

Ensuring Equity and Opportunity

The following resources will help you use lesson planning to ensure culturally relevant experiences for support children from many backgrounds.

> NAEYC's position statement "Advancing Equity in Early Childhood Education" promotes equitable learning opportunities for all children: NAEYC.org/resources/position-statements/equity

> To learn more about teachers' experiences promoting equity in the classroom, see NAEYC's Equity topic page: NAEYC.org/resources/topics/equity

> The National Council of Teachers of English offers a research policy brief, "Equity and Early Childhood Education: Reclaiming the Child," to promote culturally responsive, strengths-based, and play-based learning that honors and facilitates the linguistic strengths and developmental progress of all children: www.ncte.org/library/NCTEFiles/EquityEarlyEdBrief.pdf

> To learn more about promoting equity through anti-bias education and explore what you can do in your classroom, see NAEYC's "Anti-Bias" topic page: NAEYC.org/resources/topics/anti-bias

Enjoying Relationship-Based Teaching and Learning

Anska and Kira compare the astronauts in *To the Moon and Back,* by Jaye Garnett, and *Astronauts,* by Christiane Engel. "This one's got a string that connects to the spaceship," Anska says. "It's so they can breathe. But this guy doesn't have one." Ms. Silvie points to the illustration and remarks, "Do you see the tank strapped to the astronaut's back? In this book, the astronaut is wearing a portable tank of air so she can breathe on her spacewalk. But in this picture, the astronauts are attached to the space ship by a hose. The hose brings fresh air from the ship to the inside of their masks." Anska asks, "Do you have string? Can we tie our astronauts to their spaceship? Then they can breathe."

Ms. Silvie gets string and works carefully to tie the LEGO people to the ship. The string slips off and she tries again. Anska says, "It's okay. Sometimes you have to work at it." Ms. Silvie smiles. "Yep. Being patient is a good skill for an astronaut." The girls watch intently. Ms. Silvie says, "Now you know how astronauts breathe when they are in space." "Yep," says Kira. "They need air."

Ms. Silvie knows the girls enjoy learning about space travel. She works with the librarian to choose books and a poster. She observes the girls carefully while they are reading and talking. Ms. Silvie uses a teaching moment to answer their questions.

Respectful relationships promote learning. Respect includes noticing children's needs and responding with sensitivity as they are reading and playing. It means responding to children's questions and showing patience and encouragement.

For the last decade, an extensive body of research has documented the connection between children's relationships with their teachers and increased learning and development. Positive interactions between teachers, families, and children create a three-way foundation and set the best possible conditions for learning. Close and supportive relationships

> Create the context for learning and predict children's social skills and self-regulation as well as school readiness (Graziano et al. 2016; Jones, Bub, & Raver 2013)

> Promote resilience for children with biological or environmental risk factors and have a significant positive impact on learning and development (Moen et al. 2019)

> Connect teachers and families together to strengthen layers of resources and experiences that give children success (Nitecki 2015)

You have great influence on children's learning when you

> Listen carefully to children's play and introduce ideas and conversations to boost learning.

> Talk with children about their families and events they experience at home.

> Encourage children to tell stories and create artwork that reflects family lives and experiences.

> Plan learning themes and lesson plans with families and ask for participation in classroom ideas, activities and events, book reading, and information sharing.

> Decide which aspects of children's learning should be shared with families in daily exchanges, newsletters, and conferences.

> Support children using specific strategies you learned from families.

> Focus observations on a child's particular attribute because a family member has asked you to encourage this skill.

> Share authentic assessment documentation and explain children's progress to families.

> Discuss the results of a screening and encourage families to seek additional information and support.

> Choose items for classroom display that communicate to families what children have been learning.

> Select materials for play areas that reflect what children experience in the home and community.

> Talk about families with colleagues and brainstorm positive solutions to meet children's needs.

> Use family sayings, stories, and experiences to illustrate the meaning of new vocabulary words and connect new ideas to children's lives.

Your moment-by-moment decisions, actions, and words provide much more than a safe and happy place to learn. The message you convey has a significant impact on children's perceptions of themselves as learners and contributors to the classroom. "When children see their worth reflected in the face, words and actions of the people who surround them, they understand their worth in relation to these connections" (Fox 2019, 10).

TIPS FOR TEACHING

Communicating with Colleagues

Productive communication with colleagues influences your planning and teaching. Your success depends on mutual beliefs, commitments, mindsets, and dispositions that impact your daily decisions. To make each day go smoothly, you rely on trust and collaboration. You check in frequently to discuss how things are working. You share the responsibility to ensure each child receives appropriate support, stimulation, and care. Each of you depends on the feedback and insight of the other to evaluate the effectiveness of your planning and teaching.

To effectively plan lessons and manage the busy dynamics of the classroom, you must share similar expectations about what is going to happen. How will tasks be coordinated? Which responsibilities will be shared? How will you keep children engaged as you transition to new activities? Which children will each of you support for security and comfort? You need to be sensitive to the children and to each other, noticing what is needed on a moment-to-moment basis. The following strategies will make your communication positive and productive:

1. **Use objective language.** When you want input or feedback to help you better understand a challenge or you want to try something new, don't criticize your progress. Simply share what you have done and ask for additional ideas. "I have been putting counting objects in the math center and asking children to match objects with pictures. What else can I add that will inspire better math play?"

2. **Get feedback frequently.** When you begin adding to your lesson plan, make it a collaborative effort. "I wrote two new activities and listed the materials and questions. But when I tried it, I left out a step. What do you do to keep yourself on track with your plans?" Learning from others yields great ideas and makes teaching more fun.

3. **Ask for help.** When you are working with other adults in the classroom, it takes planning to switch gears, try a new activity, or add different strategies. Try jumpstarting the conversation. For example, "I like the way our transitions have been going, but I wonder if we can add a new song. What do you think? Will you help me do it?" Or, "I watched a video about math talk and saw how specifically the teachers asked children to describe shapes. Will you listen and see if you think we can do the same thing?" You'll have a much better chance of success when you get the support of others.

4. **Stick to the present.** When you need to address a challenge or problem, it's not necessary to bring up the past. Simply describe what you saw happen today. "I noticed that the children didn't respond well to the materials in housekeeping. I wonder if rotating in some new ones would help? What did you notice?" Getting the conversation going is easy when you focus on an event or incident that just happened. This approach helps you move quickly to effective solutions.

5. **Take notes.** Lesson plans are the perfect place to write notes about what to do next time. At the end of the day, describe what worked well. Make a list of things you want to do differently next time. For example, "Put out books ahead of time," "Print questions on a four-by-six-inch card," or "Add more challenging materials to ensure engagement." Tell your coteacher or colleagues that you are taking notes, and ask what they would suggest for next time. Their input will be invaluable to your teaching.

Setting Goals, Establishing Priorities, and Sharing Progress

> Carley's mother, Loretta, explains, "Carley and her sister were in the same program since they were babies. When we moved across the state, I worried that Carley would be in pre-K, while Camilla would be in another program. Do you think Carley is at the same level as the other children? Is she doing okay?"
>
> Carley's teacher, Ms. Elia, responds thoughtfully. "I can understand your concern. It is helpful for siblings to be together as they come and go from a program. The move was a big change for all of you. Here in the classroom, Carley fits right in. You can see how she joins the children to play. Carley is beginning to point to and recognize letters. When we meet next week, I'll show you her story and drawing about horses. She's eager for you to see it."

Ms. Elia's goal is to reassure Loretta that Carley is adjusting well to the classroom setting. She knows that with the move and change of schools, Loretta is unsure whether the new program matches Carley's previous school. After talking with Ms. Elia, Loretta feels confident about Carley's progress. Ms. Elia plans to share more information at the family conference.

When you meet with families, you may feel that you have a smorgasbord of ideas with more items you'd like to talk about than can fit into a brief conversation. How do you decide what to share and what to keep to yourself? What is important for families to know about children's learning? How can a lesson plan help you communicate better with families?

The purpose of a conference with families is to exchange information about children. You'll share what's happening in the classroom, find out what's happening at home, and celebrate new steps each child has taken. You'll identify areas where children need additional support. You'll describe the child's progress using strengths-based language and share ways you are supporting emerging skills. When you regularly share weekly lesson plans with families, these provide a context and anchor for meaningful communication.

Families are invested in their children and want to feel this time with you is about affirming and celebrating growth. All information can be shared from a strengths-based perspective, even when an area of development needs focused support. You will affirm for families that every child is unique, that skills emerge in expected patterns, and that some areas of development leap ahead of others at times. You'll remind them that progress from age 3 to 5 can be asynchronistic and that skills will integrate and stabilize over time as language, regulation, and physical coordination develop.

The most important message is that you are fully committed to children's well-being, success as learners, and adjustment to the group setting. The secondary message is that you and the family are partners in supporting children's growth in every area, and that you depend on the family's time with you to be able to know children fully and provide the best possible support. You'll identify special skills, interests, and topics about which the child is enthusiastic. When there are developmental concerns, you'll have set steps to gather information and defined shared goals for support. Families should leave feeling encouraged and reassured about the progress their child is making.

Areas of Development and Learning

Organize time with families by using areas of development and learning. You'll want to give an update on social-emotional learning, language and literacy, math concepts, science, social studies, personal development, physical development, health and nutrition, and creative arts. Families want to hear about what children have been learning, so it's helpful to summarize the projects, activities, and themes covered since your last meeting. Show families items from children's portfolios that document their accomplishments. Importantly, show families progress children have made over time.

For physical development, share positive statements that let families understand children's strengths and emerging skills; for example, "I notice Jane has developed greater confidence trying new activities outside. She is very coordinated with the Hula-Hoops and is enthusiastic about swinging and going down the slides." As you share a specific area, ask, "What do you notice about Jane's physical development at home? What do you see as her strengths and challenges?" Take notes, so that families understand you are documenting their contributions.

For personal development, say, "Jane takes pride in putting things away in her cubbie. She still gets frustrated putting on her coat, but you should see her excitement when she zips it independently. Tell me about what you see her doing at home." The information families give you will help you know how to better support children. By asking what families see at home, they may introduce to you an area of concern—or a skill for which they would like your support. This is a wonderful way to remove fear of judgement and to keep the focus on progress made. This way, you can say, "I'd love to work with Jane on reading for longer periods of time (or putting her things away or saying please and thank you)." In most cases, families will bring to your attention areas where children's development or progress needs extra support. Be sure to ask them about strengths and interests, as well.

When children's development is asynchronistic, sometimes families ask questions like, "I am worried she's not talking as much as other children," "I notice he's super energetic and has trouble calming down," or "Do you think there is something I should be concerned about related to Tonya's development?" These direct questions can be answered with reassuring language and by providing objective information.

For a family's question about language, you can respond, "I see Daria making progress in this area. Let me keep an eye on this for the next few weeks, and we can discuss it again next time we meet." Unless you have already discussed the issue with the family and have already collected data, it's best to set an action plan to observe the child carefully. If you are certain, you can say, "I find that Daria interacts well with children and is very good at expressing herself to me." If you are unsure or the family's concern raises a question in your thinking, you can simply say, "Thank you so much for asking. I'll document some of Daria's responses, so you can see the way she interacts in a group setting."

Most school districts and programs require early screening for all preschool children. If you are working in a program where children have not yet been screened and the family would like more information immediately, it's appropriate to refer the family to their pediatrician, who can address areas of development. If you feel the child would benefit from additional screening, the recommendation should be presented to families only after you have collected objective data, with evidence to show families what you observe. Most often, families will bring to your attention their concerns about development, and you can work together to set a plan. You will follow the guidelines of your program, school, or organization.

When the family asks if they should be concerned about an area of development, thank them for their question. Next, say, "Tell me more about this. What is it you see at home or outside of school that concerns you?" Then say, "Is there something specific you would like me to do to support at school?" It may be tempting to jump in and "come up with" a plan that you will tell families. Instead, always ask them what they would like you to do. Usually, they have specific ideas that you can incorporate.

In most cases, you can reassure families that you do not see their concern as a challenge for the child in the group setting. When you do see an area of development as a challenge for the child, explain your approach: "We know that behavior and learning often need shared support. Sometimes children need support for verbal or social skills. Sometimes, they need support with self-regulation or organizational skills. Each of these skills can be strengthened. We'll work together to support your child's increasing competence." When behaviors need support, work on one skill at a time and be specific. For example, you might say, "We'll support Archie to stay at the table for five minutes during meals, and you can do the same at home," or "We'll encourage Jaden's interest in reading here, and you can read to him a few minutes each day at home."

When there are ongoing areas of development that continue to be a concern, first be sure all action steps have been taken to adjust the setting, level of support, and materials. Second, establish the expectation that discussing early intervention services is a program norm. When you regularly share information with all families related to early intervention services, vision and hearing screenings, and other developmental support resources, you establish the mindset that these services are important for all families. Highlight several community programs each month and regularly distribute flyers and printed information to all families. Then, when you share or reshare this information during family meetings, the information won't come as a surprise. Resources like the Child Find Project offer public awareness materials for families and bulk materials that can be used and distributed by programs. See www.childfind-idea-il. us/About.aspx.

When you have already documented children's progress and followed the procedures for an individualized education program (IEP), the conference with families should follow the same steps. You will share progress made, affirm unique and positive traits, and discuss support for skill development. Gathering information from families, asking questions, and including their ideas and suggestions are important ingredients for success.

Before you leave the meeting, thank families for their commitment and investment in their child. Thank them for talking with you. Assure them that you will do everything possible to support their child's development and learning. Be sure to set a time to revisit any specific issues at a follow-up meeting. Express that you look forward to seeing the family at the next regular meeting.

All families should know the best method and time to contact you. As families leave, be sure to give them your contact information and the date of the next conference. They may already have this information but will appreciate the reminder. You want to convey that family communication is essential for successful teaching. Arranging the sequence of your conference around the areas of your lesson planning is a wonderful way to make that happen.

Program leadership can prioritize family engagement and offer welcoming, inclusive opportunities for family participation, including family meetings. During orientation to the program, families should learn that participation is an essential part of their child's successful learning experience. When families feel welcomed to program and classroom activities, regular teacher meetings align with this relationship-based approach. For more information about strengthening family engagement, see Masterson et al. (2019).

Self-Regulation and Behavior

Understanding the context in which children learn is essential for your communication with families. When families ask about children's behavior, focus, or energy level, the first step is to encourage healthy lifestyle habits, including active exercise, healthy nutrition, adequate sleep, and media limits. These factors impact children's ability to function well and make the most of their time in the classroom. Share weekly tips so that families know children's health is your top priority.

More than half of US children do not get the needed amount of physically active play (AAP 2018c). Research shows the need for two or more hours of vigorous exercise daily, with outdoor play promoting more active play than indoor settings (AAP, n.d.). Young children need at least three hours of active play each day or 15 minutes per hour in group settings (Pate & O'Neill 2012). Multiple studies show the positive impact of adequate vigorous exercise on children's self-regulation and learning while reducing inattention and impulsivity (Cerrillo-Urbina et al. 2015; Honig 2019; Pan 2018).

In addition to exercise, children need adequate sleep, nutrition, and stimulation. The sleep recommendations for children three to five years of age are 10 to 13 hours every 24 hours (including naps) for optimal health (AAP 2016a). Growing evidence supports the need to protect children from food colorings, chemical additives, and byproducts that may negatively impact their development and behavior (AAP 2018a). Focus on healthy modeling, with nutritious meals and snacks that include vegetables and fruit, dairy or dairy substitutes, whole grain products, and proteins. The U.S. Department of Agriculture (USDA) provides nutrition standards that encourage healthy fats and low sugar choices. Finally, children need a classroom setting that provides adequate stimulation for cognitive and language needs.

Adequate language nutrition is essential to promote learning, social skills, and cognitive development (Zauche et al. 2016). When children are well rested and can engage in a variety of meaningful learning experiences, they adjust well to group settings.

Encourage families to limit children's exposure to media. Recommendations for children ages three through five are a maximum of one hour per day of high-quality programing (AAP 2018b). Viewing at home should take place with families present to co-engage and discuss content. The American Academy of Pediatrics (2016b) states that, "It is important to emphasize to parents that the higher-order thinking skills and executive functions essential for school success, such as task persistence, impulse control, emotion regulation, and creative, flexible thinking, are best taught through unstructured and social (not digital) play, as well as responsive parent-child interactions." (2)

In preschool classrooms, additional restrictions may be set by state licensing standards that limit total media exposure to 30 minutes total per week. Media should be turned off unless used with purpose, must not be used during meals, and should be removed at least one hour before nap time (AAP, APHA, & NRC 2019). Because excessive media use and content undermine children's language, social, and regulatory development and negatively impact behavior, media should not be used to calm children. These guidelines do not limit digital media use for children with special health care needs who require and consistently use assistive and adaptive computer technology.

Child-centered lesson planning is part of a holistic approach to teaching that is designed to meet children's cognitive, social, emotional, physical, and language needs. Daily schedules and teaching activities should support children's health and well-being and create an environment with optimal supports for success. The more you know, the more you can design play spaces, routines, and interactions that effectively engage children. Anchoring teaching with a deep knowledge of children's development and understanding its context can help you communicate meaningfully with families.

Building Family Engagement Using Lesson Plans

Marley's grandfather looks with interest at the lesson plans clipped to the classroom door. He tells Ms. Janis, "I see you are identifying back yard animals and their habitats. I'd love to show the children how to build a bird house. I have materials and can come any afternoon next week." Ms. Janis answers, "Tuesday will be perfect, if that's good for you. I'll be sure to have bird identification books ready and will bring bird seed." Marley's mom hears the conversation and says, "Oh, don't buy bird seed. I have several bags at home. I'll drop them off on Monday.

Marley jumps up and down. "We are making a bird feeder!" His grandfather replies, "I'm coming to your classroom next week. We'll build and hang a new feeder. You can help me carry the wood and tools."

When you share daily lesson plans, families are aware of what's happening in the classroom and can connect in practical ways. Ms. Janis has family members that demonstrate painting, knitting, and science experiments. Grandparents come regularly to read. Her own father visits each fall to demonstrate lawn and gardening tools and explain how they work. Her classroom is a lively place where families pitch in to create meaningful experiences for the children.

Strategies for Sharing Lesson Plans

There are many ways to share your lesson plans and activities with families. In addition to printed information, you have a variety of digital options to disseminate information, such as a password-protected classroom website or social media page. You may have a secure blog where you communicate with families and post photos and videos of classroom activities. Using email, you can share current and upcoming plans.

Many digital apps allow for detailed sharing of daily, weekly, and monthly plans. Some are produced by curriculum companies and allow you to post portfolios, photos, videos, and integrated assessment tools. You'll be able to share newsletters, lesson plans, and other information with ease.

Other family communication apps offer secure communication. These allow you to share lesson plans, daily reports, emergency information, attendance records, and photo, video, and digital files. Some apps provide technology for face-to-face video calling. Some act as scheduling assistants and host information sharing with message, photo, and document uploads.

The following are some additional strategies that invite families to stay informed and contribute to children's learning.

Sharing a calendar. Create a calendar for the year with important dates, activities, and family events. Include monthly focus concepts and themes. Add tips for learning at home and invitations for families to participate in the classroom and program. Announce projects for which you'd like families to donate materials, such as empty cartons or cardboard tubes. Adding this information to the calendar helps families plan ahead. Your calendar will grow with you, reflecting the way your teaching changes over time.

Weekly summary sheets. Prepare a summary sheet for each week that includes books, topics or themes, the learning goals of interest centers (e.g., play goals), new vocabulary, and a list of special projects or materials the children will explore each day. You can organize the summary sheet by content or learning area as you add the details.

Lesson plans. Clip daily lesson plans to the door for families to view when they pick up and drop off children. This allows families to ask children questions about a day's activities. (Posted lesson plans should not include hand-written reflection notes or individualization goals for specific children.) You want families to know what children are learning and understand how they are learning it.

Activities for children at home. Add a "family learning connection" to the bottom of each lesson plan. Whether the lesson involves child-led play, shared or emergent projects, or teacher-directed activities, families will appreciate extensions, projects, and activities they can introduce at home. Consider what families can do with the materials and settings where they live. Weekly "learning connections" may jumpstart new traditions for families while extending the learning you want to reinforce. Here are ways to encourage family engagement across content areas:

› **Manners, social skills, and personal development.** Provide positive guidance tips, manners for the week, and conversation starters. For example, when children are learning to ask questions to learn about others, share the questions with families, like "What are you working on?," "What did you see on the way home?," and "What are you playing?" Families may encourage children to ask questions as well. Provide a list of books where characters model positi\ve social skills. Great resources for families include *101 Principles for Positive Guidance with Young Children: Creating Responsive Teachers*, by Katharine Kersey and Marie Masterson, and *Enjoying the Parenting Roller Coaster: Nurturing and Empowering Your Children Through the Ups and Downs*, by Marie Masterson and Katharine Kersey. These are packed with practical strategies and information for supporting children's development at home.

› **Book lists and reading.** Share the list along with related questions to engage children's thinking. Provide author websites, like Mem Fox, Susan Middleton Elya, Jan Brett, Eric Carle, Roald Dahl, Tomie DePaola, Robert Munsch, and Laura Numeroff. If you find children enjoy a specific author, provide information and websites to families.

› **Vocabulary development.** Provide a weekly word list and ask families to use the words in conversation. For example, provide a vocabulary word and sentence, like "*Beautiful.* The sunset is beautiful." Ask families to introduce additional words that express the same idea. For example, *gorgeous*, *lovely*, *stunning*, and *exquisite* are words for *beautiful*. For another example, "An elephant is big. Other words for *big* include *enormous*, *gigantic*, *huge*, *immense*, and *massive*."

› **Science and social studies concepts.** Ask families to help children collect natural objects for a child's investigation or to add to an existing classroom collection. Encourage families to play "I spy" during neighborhood walks to teach children about breeds of dogs, types of birds, names for vehicles, or types of community helpers. Provide informational books and resources for exploration.

› **Writing skills.** Ask families to write stories children dictate. They can use writing for practical purposes to make lists, to write a note to a grandmother, or to capture the story of a weekend event.

› **Math concepts in daily life.** Encourage families to ask children to count napkins and silverware to set the table. Encourage simple math story problems, such as "If Aunt Tilley comes over, how many chairs will we need?" or "How many feet do Spotty and Fluffy have together? How many tails?" At the grocery store, ask families to involve children in counting fruit and produce. Provide math and counting games that extend what children are learning in the classroom.

› **Loose parts play.** Loose parts are open-ended materials that children can connect, design, put together, arrange, stack, or explore. Share with families the skills children learn while exploring, sorting, arranging, and describing collections of objects, like invention, creative thinking, critical problem solving, and math, language, fine motor, and artistic skills. Loose parts can include natural collections, like bark, stones, seed pods, pinecones, and small branch bits; or they can be manufactured, such as paper tubes, wood scraps, wire, empty containers, nuts and bolts, fabric, ribbon, twine, and tools.

› **Creative projects for expression and inspiration.** Share ideas with families for creative projects and play children will enjoy. Families can adhere newspaper to a wall and place tempera paint on a small table to function as an easel. Share the songs, chants, and finger plays that children enjoy in the classroom. Provide weblinks for different genres of music to encourage listening and responding at home. Include a list of local community experiences like children's theater, dance, music, and arts events to encourage children's engagement in the creative arts.

In materials and suggestions you share with families, you can also provide links for museum websites, such as the American Museum of Natural History and the Smithsonian Institution, that feature activities for children. *National Wildlife*, *Ranger Rick*, and NASA Science for Kids provide age-appropriate activities and information. Inspire engagement with parks, libraries, and learning events. Your support promotes families' enthusiasm and engagement in their children's learning.

Ask families for suggested materials, activities, books, and resources related to topics you plan to study. As you engage in emergent curriculum, invite family members to share their areas of expertise. Invite families to share learning projects, discoveries, community events, and books they enjoy. Include information about what is happening in newsletters, on your classroom website, and in monthly updates. Two-way communication increases children's enrichment and establishes that learning together is a natural part of life.

HELPFUL HINT

Strategies for Positive Impact

Your positive communication strengthens family confidence and trust. Families and children benefit, but the greatest benefit will be to you, as you will be able to fine-tune your planning to become more effective. The following are strategies that make the most of your conversations with families.

Use active reflection. Reflection is more than giving thought to a situation. It means being open to new insights and ways of thinking. It means being ready to take action and make adjustments based on what you discover. Reflection empowers effective teaching because ongoing evaluation ensures that you continue to be flexible and responsive to children. Reflection takes place before, during, and after conversations.

> Before you get started, set a clear goal. "What is the result I want to accomplish?"

> During conversations, ask yourself, "Am I really listening? Have I put aside my own agenda to hear what the family wants to tell me?" When

families share, ask, "Is there anything else you want me to know?" Sometimes, the most important facts come in an afterthought.

> After your time together, consider, "What went well? What could I have said or done differently?"

> Take notes with the date, time, detailed goals, follow-up steps, and plans for the next time you meet.

Be an advocate. Explore community resources to learn what is available for families. "There's a great library story time for Noah on Saturday." "I found a STEM class at the park district." "There is a pediatric group that features health topics." Make brochures available for physical and mental health, child screening, and educational services. These connections provide layers of support for children's success.

Reframe challenges as opportunities. Self-efficacy is the expectation and confidence that using effective strategies can create positive outcomes and influence children's success (Fisher & Seroussi 2018). It requires an active and intentional mindset that reframes problems as opportunities. This mindset is visible in affirming words. "This is a great opportunity for us to rethink the level of challenge Liam needs." "This is a good time for us to work together to support Kai's artistic skills." "Let's use the next few weeks to play math games with Samir. I'm confident this will have a big impact." Positive expectations lead the way to success.

Identify mutual goals. Families and you want children to be kind, caring, and resourceful. You want them to become capable and creative. Ask families, "What goals do you have for your child?" Follow up with, "What steps can we take to reach those goals?" Affirm what families share. "Thank you for telling me more about Cruz. I look forward to supporting these goals."

See through the eyes of children. When evaluating children's progress ask, "What does this experience look and feel like to the child?" "What else can I do to build this child's strengths?" "What can I do to help families to support this child's skills?" Your goal is to maximize your impact on children's health, development, and well-being.

Family Engagement for Successful Teaching

NAEYC's Principles of Effective Family Engagement (n.d.) promote family involvement in decision making and goal setting, fostering two-way communication, ensuring reciprocal relationships, providing learning activities for the home and community, inviting participation in program-level decisions and advocacy, and implementing comprehensive program-level participation. Below are two terrific resources for exploring effective family engagement:

> The NAEYC resources for family engagement in action provide ideas and practical strategies to strengthen communication: NAEYC.org/resources/topics/family-engagement

> The US Department of Health and Human Services Administration for Children and Families presents the Head Start Early Childhood Learning and Knowledge Center resources on family engagement: https://eclkc.ohs.acf.hhs.gov/browse/topic/family-engagement

Sample Lesson Plans

Family Interview Questions

As you prepare to meet with families, it helps to think about their perspectives, concerns, and hopes for their children. Consider how to invite them into a safe and welcoming space to establish mutual respect and build a shared vision for children's success. The following strategies will help you prepare for and manage the complex process of communication and strengthen early learning experiences for children and families.

Review foundational information. Information related to health, such as identified allergies, special needs, medical issues, medication, and special routines, are essential to teaching; however, these are generally required at program enrollment. For state and federally funded programs, a home language survey, developmental screening information, initial evaluation for special education, residency, homeless status, and child welfare involvement are also part of documentation. This information provides important context as you plan effective support for the adjustment and success of each child.

Keep a record of communication. While a written or online survey can be given to families, asking each question in person is essential. Take notes about your conversations, the date you spoke, and the person or people with whom you talked. Detail decisions, agreements, and plans that are made. Keeping a record allows you to review and reflect on conversations and keeps track of progress made.

Protect professional confidence. While it can be tempting to develop friendships with the families you serve, maintain professional boundaries that will enhance your work. Staying objective and modeling confidentiality will pay off in everything you do. Importantly, you will build trust and help families feel you are "on the same page" as you invest in each child's learning

Below are sample materials for communicating with families. The Family Interview Questions (Figure 6.1) and Weekly Summary Sheet (Figure 6.2) demonstrate how to share what children are learning in the classroom. These resources can be added to your own approaches or modified to incorporate your personal creativity and focus. The family questions are designed to encourage meaningful conversation and provide families with a variety of ways to tell you about their child. The summary sheet presents active steps for families to support children's learning at home. Effective written communication with families can be concise and to the point, yet packed with helpful inspiration and ideas they can use. The more you know, the more you can strengthen lesson planning and teaching with family engagement.

Family Interview Questions

Child's name	
Family member	
Date	

- ☐ Tell me about your child. What do you notice about his/her strengths and emerging skills?

- ☐ What favorite activities does your child enjoy with the family?

- ☐ Who are the important people in your child's life?

- ☐ In what responsibilities or expectations does the child participate at home?

- ☐ What favorite books, characters, dress-up activities, or games engage your child's interest?

- ☐ What learning goals do you have for your child? What skills, strengths, and talents do you want me to encourage?

- ☐ Are there specific behaviors or interests you want me to watch for, notice, or reinforce?

- ☐ Do you have any concerns about your child's learning or development?

- ☐ What changes at home or other circumstances should I know about to be sensitive to and supportive of your child?

- ☐ Is there anything else you want me to know or support in your child's development and learning?

Additional Notes

Figure 6.1. Family Interview Questions. These questions are designed to encourage meaningful conversation with families about their children.

Weekly Summary Sheet

Weekly Summary Sheet 4/15

This week we are exploring the work of community helpers. Our goal is to help children think about safety, health, and well-being, and how community members work together to take care of each other. Children will learn about goods (products) people make and services they give. They will identify differences and similarities among workers.

Standards

PK.SOC.3d: Recognizes that all children and adults have roles, rights, and responsibilities at home, at school, and in the community.

PK.SOC.3b: Recognizes that people depend on community helpers to provide goods and services.

PK.AC.2a: Asks questions related to an item, event, or experience.

Family Focus

This week, look for community helpers with your child. You may see a baker or produce manager at the supermarket. You may watch the bus driver on your way downtown. Spend a few minutes observing.

Next, ask your child three questions:

1. What jobs does this person do?

2. What responsibilities does this person have?

3. Who benefits from or is helped by this person's work?

Attached is a card sequencing activity for the book *Fire! ¡Fuego! Brave Bomberos*, by Susan Middleton Elya.

Ask your child to retell the story while pointing to the pictures.

Classroom Focus

Monday/Book: *Fire! ¡Fuego! Brave Bomberos*, by Susan Middleton Elya.
Dramatic play concepts: Using courage to save pets. Using planning to work with partners.
Vocabulary: *courage, "at your service," sacrifice, caution, safety, teamwork, protector, extinguish.*

Tuesday/Book: *Delivering Your Mail*, by Ann Owen.
Dramatic play concepts: Sorting and delivering mail. Making labels and purchasing stamps. Sending letters and packages to families.
Vocabulary: *sort, route, carry, deliver, cart, message.*

Wednesday/Book: *Community Helpers at the Hospital*, by Mari Schuh.
Dramatic play concepts: Checking into the hospital. Giving and receiving care. Learning about health and safety.
Vocabulary: *doctor, nurse, paramedic, patient, X-ray, volunteer, gift shop, recover.*

Thursday/Book: *Frida Kahlo and Her Animalitos*, by Monica Brown.
Dramatic play concepts: Artists document and tell stories about community and family life using pictures.
Vocabulary: *document, spider monkey, parrot, fawn, turtle, turkey, heritage, Mexico City.*

Friday/Book: *Jalapeño Bagels*, by Natasha Wing.
Dramatic play concepts: Food connects us to our families and friends. Food creates happy memories and strengthens bodies. Community bakers feed people food for meals and celebrations.
Vocabulary: *pan dulce/Mexican sweet bread, empanadas de calbaza/pumpkin turnovers, batch, ingredients, knead, mixture.*

Figure 6.2. Weekly Summary Sheet. This sheet is one method for communicating with families about what children are learning in class. (Standards from NYSED [2019].)

NAEYC Standard 1—Relationships documents the necessary competencies for practice. Standard 1.A—Building Positive Relationships Between Teachers and Families underscores the critical importance of the relationship between teachers and families, with the need for ongoing communication and sensitivity to family diversity. Necessary elements include learning about children's needs, understanding how families define their race, culture, religion, home language, and family structure, keeping families informed about children's progress, learning from families about the child's experiences at home, and sharing practical information about routines, rules, and expectations.

Standard 7—Families includes three areas: 7.A, Knowing and Understanding the Program's Families; 7.B, Sharing Information Between Staff and Families; and 7.C, Nurturing Families as Advocates for Their Children. The standard states, "The truest partnership between programs and families occurs when program staff share their professional knowledge and experience with families in ways that empower family members to effectively advocate for their children's needs" (NAEYC 2018, 96).

Standard 8—Community Relationships focuses on connections with the community that enhance teaching, program vitality, and family strengths. These include information for families who need culturally or linguistically specialized services and links to resources that support children's learning and development. Standard 8.8 explains how to expand classroom boundaries to enrich curriculum and through connections with a community's cultural, business, social, and educational resources.

By integrating the resources and strengths of families, your lesson planning and teaching will change. Effective communication with families will allow you to support children in more meaningful ways. You'll be able to individualize lesson planning to ensure every child can be successful. Your teaching will be transformed as you create effective lesson plans and revitalize your classroom with child-centered teaching.

REFLECTION QUESTIONS

1. What strategies do you find are most effective when you talk with families?

2. What challenges do you encounter when discussing specific areas of development or learning that need additional support? What have you learned about the needs of families during this process?

3. How will you use the strategies from this chapter to connect more meaningfully with families?

References

Introduction

Encyclopedia Britannica, s.v. "machine." n.d. Accessed October 1, 2020. www.britannica.com/technology/machine.

NAEYC. 2018. "NAEYC Early Learning Program Accreditation Standards and Assessment Items." Washington, DC: NAEYC. www.naeyc.org/accreditation/early-learning/standards.

NAEYC. 2020. "Developmentally Appropriate Practice." Position statement. Washington, DC: NAEYC. www.naeyc.org/resources/position-statements/dap.

Chapter 1: Setting a Foundation for Teaching

Administration for Children and Families, Office of Child Care. n.d. "Ratios and Group Sizes." Accessed October 1, 2020. www.childcare.gov/index.php/consumer-education/ratios-and-group-sizes.

Barblett, L., M. Knaus, & C. Barratt-Pugh. 2016. "The Pushes and Pulls of Pedagogy in the Early Years: Competing Knowledges and the Erosion of Play-Based Learning." *Australasian Journal of Early Childhood* 41 (4): 36–43.

Bennett, S., A.A. Gunn, G. Gayle-Evans, E.S. Barrera & C.B. Leung. 2018. "Culturally Responsive Literacy Practices in an Early Childhood Community." *Early Childhood Education Journal* 46 (2): 241–248.

Berke, J. 2016. "The Importance of Play and So Much More: What I Learned from Bev Bos." *Exchange* 229 (May/June): 45–47.

Bornstein, M.H. 2013. "Parenting and Child Mental Health: A Cross-Cultural Perspective." *World Psychiatry* 12 (3): 258–265.

Brown, V. 2017. "Drama as Valuable Learning Medium in Early Childhood." *Arts Education Policy Review* 118 (3): 164–171.

BUILD Initiative. 2019. "Building Early Childhood Systems in a Multi-Ethnic Society: An Overview of Build's Briefs on Diversity and Equity." www.buildinitiative.org/Portals/0/Uploads/Documents/BuildingEarlyChildhoodSystemsinaMultiEthnicSociety.pdf.

Calzada, E.J., K.-Y. Huang, M. Hernandez, E. Soriano, C.F. Acra, S. Dawson-McClure, D. Kamboukos, & L. Brotman. 2015. "Family and Teacher Characteristics as Predictors of Parent Involvement in Education During Early Childhood Among Afro-Caribbean and Latino Immigrant Families." *Journal of Urban Education* 50 (7): 870–896.

CAST (Center for Applied Special Technology). 2019. "About Universal Design for Learning." www.cast.org/our-work/about-udl.html.

Chapman de Sousa, E.B. 2019. "Five Tips for Engaging Multilingual Children in Conversation." *Young Children* 74 (2): 24–31.

Cushner, K., & S.-C. Chang. 2015. "Developing Intercultural Competence Through Overseas Student Teaching: Checking Our Assumptions." *Intercultural Education* 26 (3): 165–178.

Cutter-Mackenzie, A., & S. Edwards. 2013. "Toward a Model of Early Childhood Environmental Education: Foregrounding, Developing, and Connecting Knowledge through Play-Based Learning." *Journal of Environmental Education* 44 (3): 195–213.

Degotardi, S. 2017. "Joint Attention in Infant-Toddler Early Childhood Programs: Its Dynamics and Potential for Collaborative Learning." *Contemporary Issues in Early Childhood* 18 (4): 409–421.

Dinnebeil, L.A., M.B. Boat, & Y. Bae. 2013. "Integrating Principles of Universal Design into the Early Childhood Curriculum." *Dimensions of Early Childhood* 41 (1): 3–14.

ED (US Department of Education) & HHS (US Department of Health and Human Services). 2015. "Policy Statement on Inclusion of Children with Disabilities in Early Childhood Programs." www2.ed.gov/about/inits/ed/earlylearning/inclusion/index.html.

Edwards, S. 2017. "Play-Based Learning and Intentional Teaching: Forever Different?" *Australasian Journal of Early Childhood* 42 (2): 4–11.

Foley, G.M. 2017. "Play as Regulation: Promoting Self-Regulation Through Play." *Topics in Language Disorders* 37 (3): 241–258.

Gadzikowski, A. 2016. "Everyday Differentiation: How Administrators Support Differentiation of Curriculum and Instruction in Early Childhood Classrooms." *Exchange* 227 (Jan/Feb): 12–16.

Gibbs, C. 2005. "Teachers' Cultural Self-Efficacy: Teaching and Learning in Multicultural Settings." *New Zealand Journal of Educational Studies* 40 (1/2): 101–112.

Guo, K. 2015. "Teacher Knowledge, Child Interest, and Parent Expectation: Factors Influencing Multicultural Programs in an Early Childhood Setting." *Australasian Journal of Early Childhood* 40 (1): 63–70.

Hamlin, M., & D.B. Wisneski. 2012. "Supporting the Scientific Thinking and Inquiry of Toddlers and Preschoolers Through Play." *Young Children* 67 (3): 82–88.

Hedges, H., & M. Cooper. 2018. "Relational Play-Based Pedagogy: Theorising a Core Practice in Early Childhood Education." *Teachers and Teaching* 24 (4): 369–383.

Jacobsen, W.C., G.T. Pace, & N.G. Ramirez. 2019. "Punishment and Inequality at an Early Age: Exclusionary Discipline in Elementary School." *Social Forces* 97 (3): 973–998.

Julius, G.D. 2018. "Dual-Language Learners: An Emerging Topic of Research that All Educators Should Watch." *Exchange* 243 (Sept/Oct): 55–58.

Karabon, A. 2017. "They're Lovin' It: How Preschool Children Mediated Their Funds of Knowledge into Dramatic Play." *Early Child Development and Care* 187 (5/6): 896–909.

Kinsner, K. 2019. "Rocking and Rolling. Fresh Air, Fun, and Exploration: Why Outdoor Play Is Essential for Healthy Development." *Young Children* 74 (2): 90–92.

Kucharczyk, S., M.A. Sreckovic, & T.R. Schultz. 2019. "Practical Strategies to Promote Reflective Practice When Working with Young Children with and At-Risk for Disabilities." *Early Childhood Education Journal* 47 (3): 343–352.

Lillard, A.S., M.D. Learner, E.J. Hopkins, R.A. Dore, E.C. Smith, & C.M. Palmquist. 2013. "The Impact of Pretend Play on Children's Development: A Review of the Evidence." *Psychological Bulletin* 139 (1): 1–34.

Lohmann, M. 2017. "Preparing Young Children for the Inclusion of Children with Disabilities into the Classroom." *NAEYC* (blog), July 25. www.naeyc.org/resources/blog/preparing-young-children-inclusion.

Madrid Akpovo, S. 2019. "Uncovering Cultural Assumptions: Using a Critical Incident Technique During an International Student-Teaching Field Experience." *Contemporary Issues in Early Childhood* 20 (2): 146–162.

Massing, C., A. Kirova, & K. Henning. 2013. "The Role of First Language Facilitators in Redefining Parent Involvement: Newcomer Families' Funds of Knowledge in an Intercultural Preschool Program." *Canadian Children* 38 (2): 4–13.

McKee, A., & D. Friedlander. 2017. "Access, Accommodation, and Attitude." *Exchange* 235 (May/June): 88–94.

NAEYC. 2018. "NAEYC Early Learning Program Accreditation Standards and Assessment Items." Washington, DC: NAEYC. www.naeyc.org/accreditation/early-learning/standards.

NAEYC. 2020. "Developmentally Appropriate Practice." Position statement. Washington, DC: NAEYC. www.naeyc.org/resources/position-statements/dap.

Nilsson, M., B. Ferholt, & R. Lecusay. 2018. "'The Playing-Exploring Child': Reconceptualizing the Relationship Between Play and Learning in Early Childhood Education." *Contemporary Issues in Early Childhood* 19 (3): 231–245.

Peguero, A.A., Z. Shekarkhar, A.M. Popp, & D.J. Koo. 2015. "Punishing the Children of Immigrants: Race, Ethnicity, Generational Status, Student Misbehavior, and School Discipline." *Journal of Immigrant and Refugee Studies* 13 (2): 200–220.

Rasaol, C., J. Eklund, & E.M. Hansen. 2011. "Toward a Conceptualization of Ethnocultural Empathy." *Journal of Social, Evolutionary, and Cultural Psychology* 5 (1): 1–13.

Siraj-Blatchford, I. 2009. "Conceptualizing Progression in the Pedagogy of Play and Sustained Shared Thinking in Early Childhood Education: A Vygotskian Perspective." *Educational and Child Psychology* 26 (2): 77–89.

Spiewak Toub, T., B. Hassinger-Das, K.T. Nesbitt, H. Ilgaz , D.S. Weisberg , K. Hirsh-Pasek, R.M. Golinkoff, A. Nicolopoulou, & D.K. Dickinson. 2018. "The Language of Play: Developing Preschool Vocabulary Through Play Following Shared Book-Reading." *Early Childhood Research Quarterly* 45 (4): 1–17.

Velez-Ibanez, C.G. 1988. "Networks of Exchange Among Mexicans in the U.S. and Mexico: Local Level Mediating Responses to National and International Transformations." *Urban Anthropology* 17 (1): 27–51.

Watts-Taffe, S., B.P. Laster, L. Broach, B. Marinak, C. McDonald Connor, & Doris Walker-Dalhouse, 2012. "Differentiated Instruction: Making Informed Teacher Decisions." *Reading Teacher* 66 (4): 303–314.

Whittingham, C.E., E.B. Hoffman, & J.C. Rumenapp. 2018. "It Ain't 'Nah' It's 'No'": Preparing Preschoolers for the Language of School." *Journal of Early Childhood Literacy* 18 (4): 465–489.

Whorrall, J., & S.Q. Cabell. 2016. "Supporting Children's Oral Language Development in the Preschool Classroom." *Early Childhood Education Journal* 44 (4): 335–341.

Wolf, E. 1966. *Peasants*. Englewood Cliffs, NJ: Prentice-Hall.

Yogman, M., A. Garner, J. Hutchinson, K. Hirsh-Pasek, & R.M. Golinkoff. 2018. "The Power of Play: A Pediatric Role in Enhancing Development in Young Children." *Pediatrics* 142 (3): 1–16.

Chapter 2: Making Lesson Planning Work for You

Bakker, A. 2018. "Discovery Learning: Zombie, Phoenix, or Elephant?" *Instructional Science* 46 (1): 169–183.

Blake, S. 2009. "Engage, Investigate, and Report: Enhancing the Curriculum with Scientific Inquiry." *Young Children* 64 (6): 49–53.

Cheatham, G.A., M. Jimenez-Silva, & H. Park. 2015. "Teacher Feedback to Support Oral Language Learning for Young Dual Language Learners." *Early Child Development and Care* 185 (9): 1452–1463.

Echevarría, J., M. Vogt, & D. Short. 2017. *Making Language Comprehensible for English Learners: The SIOP Model*. 5th ed. Boston: Allyn and Bacon.

Ertürk Kara, H.G., M.S. Gönen, & R. Pianta. 2017. "The Examination of the Relationship Between the Quality of Teacher-Child Interaction and Children's Self-Regulation Skills." *Hacettepe University Journal of Education* 32 (4): 880–895.

Espinosa, L.M. 2018. "Encouraging the Development and Achievement of Dual Language Learners in Early Childhood." *American Educator* 42 (3): 10–11, 39.

Fleer, M. 2010. "The Re-Theorisation of Collective Pedagogy and Emergent Curriculum." *Cultural Studies of Science Education* 5 (3): 563–576.

Hall-Kenyon, K.M., & A.A. Rosborough. 2017. "Exploring Pedagogical Relationships in the Context of Free Play." *Early Years* 37 (3): 326–337.

Hassinger-Das, B., K. Hirsh-Pasek, & R.M. Golinkoff. 2017. "The Case of Brain Science and Guided Play: A Developing Story." *Young Children* 72 (2): 45–50.

Hirsh-Pasek, K., R.M. Golinkoff, L.E. Berk, & D. Singer. 2008. *A Mandate for Playful Learning in Preschool: Presenting the Evidence*. New York: Oxford University Press.

Jones, S.M., K. Bub, & C.C. Raver. 2013. "Unpacking the Black Box of the Chicago School Readiness Project Intervention: The Mediating Roles of Teacher Child Relationship Quality and Self-Regulation." *Early Education and Development* 24 (7): 1043–1064.

Lessow-Hurley, J. 2013. *The Foundations of Dual Language Instruction*. 6th ed. Upper Saddle River, NJ: Pearson.

Lindo, N.A., D.D. Taylor, K. Meany-Walen, K.E. Purswell, K.M. Jayne, T. Gonzales, & L. Jones. 2014. "Teachers as Therapeutic Agents: Perceptions of a School-Based Mental Health Initiative." *British Journal of Guidance and Counseling* 42 (3): 284–296.

Lippard, C.N., K.M. La Paro, H.L. Rouse, & D.A. Crosby. 2018. "A Closer Look at Teacher–Child Relationships and Classroom Emotional Context in Preschool." *Child and Youth Care Forum* 47 (1): 1–21.

McNally, S., & R. Slutsky. 2018. "Teacher–Child Relationships Make All the Difference: Constructing Quality Interactions in Early Childhood Settings." *Early Child Development and Care* 188 (5): 508–523.

NAEYC. 2018. "NAEYC Early Learning Program Accreditation Standards and Assessment Items." Washington, DC: NAEYC. www.naeyc.org/accreditation/early-learning/standards.

NAEYC. 2020. "Developmentally Appropriate Practice." Position statement. Washington, DC: NAEYC. www.naeyc.org/resources/position-statements/dap.

New Jersey State Department of Education. 2014. *Preschool Teaching and Learning Standards*. www.state.nj.us/education/ece/guide/standards.pdf.

Nunamaker, R.G.C., W.A. Mosier, & G. Pickett. 2017. "Promoting Inquiry-Based Science Education." *Exchange* 238 (Nov/Dec): 38–42.

Osher, D., P. Cantor, J. Berg, L. Steyer, & T. Rose. 2020. "Drivers of Human Development: How Relationships and Context Shape Learning and Development." *Applied Developmental Science* 24 (1): 6–36.

Pianta, R.C., J.E. Whittaker, V. Vitiello, A. Ansari, & E. Ruzek. 2018. "Classroom Process and Practices in Public Pre-K Programs: Describing and Predicting Educational Opportunities in the Early Learning Sector." *Early Education and Development* 29 (6): 797–813.

Rodriguez, S., K. Allen, J. Harron, & S.A. Qadri. 2019. "Making and the 5E Learning Cycle." *Science Teacher* 86 (5): 48–55.

Sawyer, B.E., P.H. Manz, K.A. Martin, T.C. Hammond, & S. Garrigan. 2016. "Teachers and Parents as Partners: Developing a Community of Practice to Support Latino Preschool Dual Language Learners." *Advances in Early Education and Day Care* 20: 159–186.

Sciaraffa, M.A., P.D. Zeanah, & C.H. Zeanah. 2018. "Understanding and Promoting Resilience in the Context of Adverse Childhood Experiences." *Early Childhood Education Journal* 46 (3): 343–353

Stipek, D. 2017. "Playful Math Instruction in the Context of Standards and Accountability." *Young Children* 72 (3): 8–12.

Trundle, K.C., & M.M. Smith. 2017. "A Hearts-on, Hands-on, Minds-on Model for Preschool Science Learning." *Young Children* 72 (1): 80–86.

Watt, S.J., W.J. Therrien, E. Kaldenberg, & J. Taylor. 2013. "Promoting Inclusive Practices in Inquiry-Based Science Classrooms." *Teaching Exceptional Children* 4 (4): 40–48.

Chapter 3: Preparing Child-Centered Themes and Play Areas

Bartlett, J.D., & K. Steber. 2019. "How to Implement Trauma-Informed Care to Build Resilience to Childhood Trauma." *Child Trends,* May 9. www.childtrends.org/publications/how-to-implement-trauma-informed-care-to-build-resilience-to-childhood-trauma

Battaglia, G., M. Alesi, G. Tabacchi, A. Palma, & M. Bellafiore. 2019. "The Development of Motor and Pre-Literacy Skills by a Physical Education Program in Preschool Children: A Non-Randomized Pilot Trial." *Frontiers in Psychology* 9 (2694). doi:10.3389/fpsyg.2018.02694.

Bluiett, T. 2018. "Ready or Not, Play or Not: Next Steps for Sociodramatic Play and the Early Literacy Curriculum: A Theoretical Perspective." *Reading Improvement* 55 (3): 83–88.

Boylan, F., L. Barblett, & M. Knaus. 2018. "Early Childhood Teachers' Perspectives of Growth Mindset: Developing Agency in Children." *Australasian Journal of Early Childhood* 43 (3): 16–24.

Broughton, A., & M.B. McClary. 2019/2020. "9X: Creating a Culturally Responsive STEAM Curriculum." *Teaching Young Children* 13 (2): 8–11.

Bustamante, A.S., & A.H. Hindman. 2019. "Classroom Quality and Academic School Readiness Outcomes in Head Start: The Indirect Effect of Approaches to Learning." *Early Education and Development* 30 (1): 19–35.

Campbell, S.B., S.A. Denham, G.Z. Howarth, S.M. Jones, J. Vick Whittaker, A.P. Williford, M.T. Willoughby, M. Yudron, & K. Darling-Churchill. 2016. "Commentary on the Review of Measures of Early Childhood Social and Emotional Development: Conceptualization, Critique, and Recommendations." *Journal of Applied Developmental Psychology* 45 (July/Aug): 19–41.

Center on the Developing Child. n.d. "Executive Function and Self-Regulation." https://developingchild.harvard.edu/science/key-concepts/executive-function.

Chatzipanteli, A., V. Grammatikopoulos, & A. Gregoriadis. 2014. "Development and Evaluation of Metacognition in Early Childhood Education." *Early Child Development and Care* 184 (8): 1223–1232.

Gerde, H.K., L.E. Skibbe, T.S. Wright, & S.N. Douglas. 2019. "Evaluation of Head Start Curricula for Standards-Based Writing Instruction." *Early Childhood Education Journal* 47 (1): 97–105.

Haimovitz, K., & C.S. Dwenk. 2017. "The Origins of Children's Growth and Fixed Mindsets: New Research and a New Proposal." *Child Development* 88 (6): 1849–1859.

Horn, E., & R. Banerjee. 2009. "Understanding Curriculum Modifications and Embedded Learning Opportunities in the Context of Supporting All Children's Success." *Language, Speech, and Hearing Services in Schools* 40 (4): 406–415.

Hughes, C.A., J.R. Morris, W.J. Therrien, & S.K. Benson. 2017. "Explicit Instruction: Historical and Contemporary Contexts." *Learning Disabilities Research and Practice* 32 (3): 140–148.

Israel, M., C. Ribuffo, & S. Smith. 2014. *Universal Design for Learning: Recommendations for Teacher Preparation and Professional Development*. Gainesville, FL: University of Florida, Collaboration for Effective Educator Development, Accountability, and Reform Center. https://ceedar.education.ufl.edu/wp-content/uploads/2014/08/IC-7_FINAL_08-27-14.pdf.

Kersey, K.C., & M.L. Masterson. 2013. *101 Principles for Positive Guidance: Creating Responsive Teachers*. Upper Saddle River, NJ: Pearson Education.

Kim, S., & R. Plotka. 2016. "Myths and Facts Regarding Second Language Acquisition in Early Childhood: Recommendations for Policymakers, Administrators, and Teachers." *Dimensions of Early Childhood* 44 (1): 18–24.

Luna, S.M. 2017. "Academic Language in Preschool: Research and Context." *Reading Teacher* 71 (1): 89–93.

McDermott, P.A., S.H. Rikoon, & J.W. Fantuzzo. 2014. "Tracing Children's Approaches to Learning Through Head Start, Kindergarten, and First Grade: Different Pathways to Different Outcomes." *Journal of Educational Psychology* 106 (1): 200–213.

Mitchell, L.C. 2004. "Making the Most of Creativity in Activities for Young Children with Disabilities." *Young Children* 59 (4): 46–49.

Mixon, C.Y. 2015. "One, Two, Three: Math as Far as the Eye Can See." *Texas Child Care* 38 (4): 25–29.

Montroy, J.J., R.P. Bowles, L.E. Skibbe, M.M. McClelland, & F.J. Morrison. 2016. "The Development of Self-Regulation Across Early Childhood." *Developmental Psychology* 52 (11): 1744–1762.

Moomaw, S. 2015. "Assessing the Difficulty Level of Math Board Games for Young Children." *Journal of Research in Childhood Education* 29 (4): 492–509.

Moreno, A.J., I. Shwayder, & I.D. Friedman. 2017. "The Function of Executive Function: Everyday Manifestations of Regulated Thinking in Preschool Settings." *Early Childhood Education Journal* 45 (2): 143–153.

NAEYC. 2020. "Developmentally Appropriate Practice." Position statement. Washington, DC: NAEYC. www.naeyc.org/resources/position-statements/dap.

Neuenschwander, R., M. Röthlisberger, P. Cimeli, & C.M. Roebers. 2012. "How Do Different Aspects of Self-Regulation Predict Successful Adaptation to School?" *Journal of Experimental Child Psychology* 113 (3): 353–371.

New Jersey State Department of Education. 2014. *Preschool Teaching and Learning Standards.* www.state.nj.us/education/ece/guide/standards.pdf.

Phillips, B.M., Y. Zhao, & M.J. Weekley. 2018. "Teacher Language in the Preschool Classroom: Initial Validation of a Classroom Environment Observation Tool." *Early Education and Development* 29 (3): 379–397.

Rademacher, A., & U. Koglin. 2019. "The Concept of Self-Regulation and Preschoolers' Social-Emotional Development: A Systematic Review." *Early Child Development and Care* 189 (14): 2299–2317.

Reed, K.E., & J. Mercer Young. 2018. "Play Games, Learn Math! Pattern Block Puzzles." *Teaching Young Children* 11 (4): 20–23.

Skibbe, L.E., H.K. Gerde, T.S. Wright, & C.R. Samples-Steele. 2016. "A Content Analysis of Phonological Awareness and Phonics in Commonly Used Head Start Curricula." *Early Childhood Education Journal* 44 (3): 225–233.

Chapter 4: Planning Teacher-Directed Activities

Alanís, I., Arreguín M., & Salinas-González, I. 2021. *The Essentials: Supporting Dual Language Learners in Diverse Environments in Preschool and Kindergarten.* Washington, DC: NAEYC.

Beecher, C.C., M.I. Abbott, S. Petersen, & C.R. Greenwood. 2017. "Using the Quality of Literacy Implementation Checklist to Improve Preschool Literacy Instruction." *Early Childhood Education Journal* 45 (5): 595–602.

Carr, R.C., I.L. Mokrova, L. Vernon-Feagans, & M.R. Burchinal. 2019. "Cumulative Classroom Quality During Pre-Kindergarten and Kindergarten and Children's Language, Literacy, and Mathematics Skills." *Early Childhood Research Quarterly* 47 (2): 218–228.

CDE (California Department of Education). 2008. *California Preschool Learning Foundations.* Vol. 1. Sacramento: CDE. www.cde.ca.gov/sp/cd/re/documents/preschoollf.pdf.

Darrow, C.L. 2013. "The Effectiveness and Precision of Intervention Fidelity Measures in Preschool Intervention Research." *Early Education and Development* 24 (8): 1137–1160

Dotterer, A.M., M. Burchinal, D. Bryant, D. Early, & R.C. Pianta. 2013. "Universal and Targeted Pre-Kindergarten Programmes: A Comparison of Classroom Characteristics and Child Outcomes." *Early Child Development and Care* 183 (7): 931–950.

Fountas, I.C., & G.S. Pinnell. 2010. *The Continuum of Literacy Learning, Grades PreK–2: A Guide to Teaching.* 2nd ed. Portsmouth, NH: Heinemann.

Flynn, E.E. 2016. "Language-Rich Early Childhood Classroom: Simple but Powerful Beginnings." *Reading Teacher* 70 (2): 159–166.

Graue, E., S. Ryan, B. Wilinski, K. Northey, & N. Amato. 2018. "What Guides Pre-K Programs?" *Teachers College Record* 120 (8): 1–36.

Gropen, J., J.F. Kook, C. Hoisington, & N. Clark-Chiarelli. 2017. "Foundations of Science Literacy: Efficacy of a Preschool Professional Development Program in Science on Classroom Instruction, Teachers' Pedagogical Content Knowledge, and Children's Observations and Predictions." *Early Education and Development* 28 (5): 607–631.

ISBE (Illinois State Board of Education). 2020. "Illinois Early Learning and Development Standards for Preschool." Springfield, IL: ISBE. www.isbe.net/Documents/early_learning_standards.pdf.

Jenkins, J.M., G.J. Duncan, A. Auger, M. Bitler, T. Domina, & M. Burchinal. 2018. "Boosting School Readiness: Should Preschool Teachers Target Skills or the Whole Child?" *Economics of Education Review* 65: 107–125.

Jenkins, J.M., A.A. Whitaker, T. Nguyen, & W. Yu. 2019. "Distinctions Without a Difference? Preschool Curricula and Children's Development." *Journal of Research on Educational Effectiveness* 12 (3): 514–549.

McGuire, P.R., M. Kinzie, K. Thunder, & R. Berry. 2016. "Methods of Analysis and Overall Mathematics Teaching Quality in At-Risk Prekindergarten Classrooms." *Early Education and Development* 27 (1): 89–109.

Pianta, R., J. Downer, & B. Hamre. 2016. "Quality in Early Education Classrooms: Definitions, Gaps, and Systems." *Future of Children* 26 (2): 119–137.

Pianta, R.C., J.E. Whittaker, V. Vitiello, A. Ansari, & E. Ruzek. 2018. "Classroom Process and Practices in Public Pre-K Programs: Describing and Predicting Educational Opportunities in the Early Learning Sector." *Early Education and Development* 29 (6): 797–813.

Tompert, A. 1997. *Grandfather Tang's Story*. New York: Crown Publishers.

Wellberg, J. 2019. "Fostering Critical Thinking in Pre-K." *Reading Teacher* 73 (3): 377.

Chapter 5: Using Observation, Documentation, and Assessment to Guide Teaching

Alanís, I., Arreguín M., & Salinas-González, I. 2021. *The Essentials: Supporting Dual Language Learners in Diverse Environments in Preschool and Kindergarten*. Washington, DC: NAEYC.

Buzzelli, C.A. 2018. "The Moral Dimensions of Assessment in Early Childhood Education." *Contemporary Issues in Early Childhood* 19 (2): 154–166.

Carley Rizzuto, K. 2017. "Teachers' Perceptions of ELL Students: Do Their Attitudes Shape Their Instruction?" *Teacher Educator* 52 (3): 182–202.

Chu, S.-Y., & S. Flores. 2011. "Assessment of English Language Learners with Learning Disabilities." *Clearing House* 84 (6): 244–248.

Jacoby, J.W., & N.K. Lesaux. 2019. "Supporting Dual Language Learners in Head Start: Teacher Beliefs About Teaching Priorities and Strategies to Facilitate English Language Acquisition." *Journal of Early Childhood Teacher Education* 40 (2): 120–137.

Kim, D.H., R.G. Lambert, S. Durham, & D.C. Burts. 2018. "Examining the Validity of GOLD with 4-Year-Old Dual Language Learners." *Early Education and Development* 29 (4): 477–493.

Mason, B.A., A.B. Gunersel, & E.A. Ney. 2014. "Cultural and Ethnic Bias in Teacher Ratings of Behavior: A Criterion-Focused Review." *Psychology in Schools* 51 (10): 1017–1030.

McConnell, S. 2019. "Measuring More Than Fun." *Language Magazine* 19 (1): 19–22.

NAEYC. 2011. "Code of Ethical Conduct and Statement of Commitment." Brochure. Rev. ed. Washington, DC: NAEYC.

NAEYC. 2018. "NAEYC Early Learning Program Accreditation Standards and Assessment Items." Washington, DC: NAEYC. www.naeyc.org/accreditation/early-learning/standards.

NAEYC. 2020. "Developmentally Appropriate
Practice." Position statement. Washington, DC:
NAEYC. www.naeyc.org/resources/position-
statements/dap.

Ntuli, E., A. Nyarambi, & M. Traore. 2014.
"Assessment in Early Childhood Education:
Threats and Challenges to Effective Assessment
of Immigrant Children." *Journal of Research in
Special Education Needs* 14 (4): 221–228.

Regenstein, E., M. Conners, R. Romero-Jurado,
& J. Weiner. 2017. "Uses and Misuses
of Kindergarten Readiness Assessment
Results." *Ounce of Prevention Fund Policy
Conversations* 6 (1): 1–48.

Rudd, T. 2014. "Racial Disproportionality in School
Discipline: Implicit Bias Is Heavily Implicated."
Kirwan Institute Issue Brief. Columbus: The
Ohio State University. http://kirwaninstitute.
osu.edu/wp-content/uploads/2014/02/racial-
disproportionality-schools-02.pdf.

Salmon, A.K. 2016. "Learning by Thinking During
Play: The Power of Reflection to Aid Performance."
Early Child Development and Care 186 (3):
480–496.

Schultz, M. 2015. "The Documentation of Children's
Learning in Early Childhood Education." *Children
in Society* 29 (3): 209–218.

Staats, C. 2014. "Implicit Racial Bias and School
Discipline Disparities: Exploring the Connection."
Kirwan Institute Special Report. Columbus: The
Ohio State University. http://kirwaninstitute.
osu.edu/wp-content/uploads/2014/05/ki-ib-
argument-piece03.pdf.

Weitzman, C. 2019. "How Can We Support
Children and Families with Information
Gleaned from Developmental Screening?"
Pediatrics 144 (6): 1–2.

Wood, C., & C. Schatschneider. 2019. "Item Bias:
Predictors of Accuracy on Peabody Picture
Vocabulary Test–Fourth Edition Items for
Spanish-English Speaking Children." *Journal of
Speech, Language, and Hearing Research* 62 (5):
1392–1402.

Chapter 6: Enriching Communication with Families and Colleagues

AAP (American Academy of Pediatrics), APHA
(American Public Health Association), & NRC
(National Resource Center for Health and Safety
in Child Care and Early Education). 2019. *Caring
for Our Children: National Health and Safety
Performance Standards; Guidelines for Early
Care and Education Programs.* 4th ed. Itasca, IL:
AAP. https://nrckids.org/files/CFOC4%20pdf-%20
FINAL.pdf.

AAP (American Academy of Pediatrics). 2016a.
"American Academy of Pediatrics Supports
Childhood Sleep Guidelines." HealthyChildren.
org, June 13. www.healthychildren.org/English/
news/Pages/AAP-Supports-Childhood-Sleep-
Guidelines.aspx.

AAP (American Academy of Pediatrics). 2016b.
"Media and Young Minds." *Pediatrics* 138 (5):
e20162591. https://pediatrics.aappublications.
org/content/138/5/e20162591.

AAP (American Academy of Pediatrics). 2018a.
"American Academy of Pediatrics Says Some
Common Food Additives May Pose Health Risks
to Children." HealthyChildren.org, July 23. www.
healthychildren.org/English/news/Pages/AAP-
Says-Some-Common-Food-Additives-May-Pose-
Health-Risks-to-Children.aspx

AAP (American Academy of Pediatrics). 2018b.
"Kids and Tech: Tips for Parents in the Digital
Age." HealthyChildren.org, last modified October
8. www.healthychildren.org/English/family-life/
Media/Pages/Tips-for-Parents-Digital-Age.aspx.

AAP (American Academy of Pediatrics). 2018c.
"Physical Activity Should Be a Vital Sign of
Children's Overall Health." https://www.
eurekalert.org/pub_releases/2018-11/aaop-
pas102318.php.

AAP (American Academy of Pediatrics). n.d. "Preschooler Physical Activity." www.aap.org/en-us/advocacy-and-policy/aap-health-initiatives/HALF-Implementation-Guide/Age-Specific-Content/Pages/Preschooler-Physical-Activity.aspx.

Beneke, M., & G.A. Cheatham. 2015. "Speaking Up for African American English: Equity and Inclusion in Early Childhood Settings." *Early Childhood Education Journal* 43 (2): 127–134.

Calzada, E.J., K.-Y. Huang, M. Hernandez, E. Soriano, C.F. Acra, S. Dawson-McClure, D. Kamboukos, & L. Brotman. 2015. "Family and Teacher Characteristics as Predictors of Parent Involvement in Education During Early Childhood Among Afro-Caribbean and Latino Immigrant Families." *Journal of Urban Education* 50 (7): 870–896.

Cerrillo-Urbina, A.J., A. García-Hermoso, M. Sánchez-López, M.J. Pardo-Guijarro, J.L. Santos Gómez, & V. Martínez-Vizcaíno. 2015. "The Effects of Physical Exercise in Children with Attention Deficit Hyperactivity Disorder: A Systematic Review and Meta-Analysis of Randomized Control Trials." *Child Care, Health, and Development* 41 (6): 779–788.

Czik, A., & K. Lewis. 2016. "Family Involvement in the Assessment and Instruction of Dual Language Learners." In *Family Involvement in Early Education and Child Care*, ed. J.A. Sutterby, 143–158. Vol. 20 of *Advances in Early Education and Day Care*. Bingley, UK: Emerald Publishing Limited.

Durand, T.M. 2011. "Latino Parental Involvement in Kindergarten: Findings from the Early Childhood Longitudinal Study." *Hispanic Journal of Behavioral Sciences* 33 (4): 469–489.

Fantuzzo, J., V. Gadsden, F. Li, F. Sproul, P. McDermott, D. Hightower, & A. Minney. 2013. "Multiple Dimensions of Family Engagement in Early Childhood Education: Evidence for a Short Form of the Family Involvement Questionnaire." *Early Childhood Research Quarterly* 28 (4): 734–742.

Fisher, Y., & K. Seroussi. 2018. "Leading an Excellent Preschool: What Is the Role of Self-Efficacy?" *Quality Assurance in Education: An International Perspective* 26 (4): 430–445.

Fox, Z. 2019. "The Power of Relationships." *Educating Young Children: Learning and Teaching in the Early Childhood Years* 25 (2): 10–11.

Galindo, C., & S.B. Sheldon. 2012. "School and Home Connections and Children's Kindergarten Achievement Gains: The Mediating Role of Family Involvement." *Early Childhood Research Quarterly* 27 (1): 90–103.

Graziano, P.A., L.R. Garb, R. Ros, K. Hart, & A. Garcia. 2016. "Executive Functioning and School Readiness Among Preschoolers with Externalizing Problems: The Moderating Role of the Student–Teacher Relationship." *Early Education and Development* 27 (5): 573–589.

Guo, K. 2015. "Teacher Knowledge, Child Interest and Parent Expectation: Factors Influencing Multicultural Programs in an Early Childhood Setting." *Australasian Journal of Early Childhood* 40 (1): 63–70.

Hedges, H., & D. Lee. 2010. "'I Understood the Complexity Within Diversity': Preparation for Partnership with Families in Early Childhood Settings." *Asia-Pacific Journal of Teacher Education* 38 (4): 257–272.

Hernandez, P.R., M. Estrada, A. Woodcock, & P.W. Schultz. 2017. "Protégé Perceptions of High Mentorship Quality Depend on Shared Values More than on Demographic Match." *The Journal of Experimental Education* 85 (3): 450–468.

Honig, A.S. 2019. "Exercise Times Enhance Child Skill Building." *Early Child Development and Care* 189 (9): 1457–1464.

Jones, S.M., K. Bub, & C.C. Raver. 2013. "Unpacking the Black Box of the Chicago School Readiness Project Intervention: The Mediating Roles of Teacher Child Relationship Quality and Self-Regulation." *Early Education and Development* 24 (7): 1043–1064.

Julius, G.D. 2017. "The Importance of Parent-Provider Relationships in Early Education." *Exchange* 237 (Sept/Oct): 48–50.

Lang, S.N., A.R. Tolbert, S. Schoppe-Sullivan, & A.E. Bonomi. 2016. "A Cocaring Framework for Infants and Toddlers: Applying a Model of Coparenting to Parent–Teacher Relationships." *Early Childhood Research Quarterly* 34 (1): 40–52.

Maríñez-Lora, A.M., & S.M. Quintana. 2009. "Low-Income Urban African-American and Latino Parents' School Involvement: Testing a Theoretical Model." *School Mental Health* 1 (4): 212–228.

Massing, C., A. Kirova, & K. Henning. 2016. "The Role of First Language Facilitators in Redefining Parent Involvement: Newcomer Families' Funds of Knowledge in an Intercultural Preschool Program." *Canadian Children* 38 (2): 4–13.

Masterson, M., M. Abel, T. Talan, & J. Bella. 2019. *Building on Whole Leadership: Energizing and Strengthening Your Early Childhood Program.* Lewisville, NC: Gryphon House.

McWayne, C., R. Campos, & M. Owsianik. 2008. "A Multidimensional, Multilevel Examination of Mother and Father Involvement Among Culturally Diverse Head Start Families." *Journal of School Psychology* 46 (5): 551–573.

Moen, A.L., S.M. Sheridan, R.E. Schumacher, & K.C. Cheng. 2019. "Early Childhood Student–Teacher Relationships What Is the Role of Classroom Climate for Children Who Are Disadvantaged?" *Early Childhood Education Journal* 47 (3): 331–341.

Mortensen, J.A., & M.A. Barnett. 2015. "Teacher–Child Interactions in Infant/Toddler Child Care and Socioemotional Development." *Early Education and Development* 26 (2): 209–229.

NAEYC. 2018. "NAEYC Early Learning Program Accreditation Standards and Assessment Items." Washington, DC: NAEYC. www.naeyc.org/accreditation/early-learning/standards.

NAEYC. 2020. "Developmentally Appropriate Practice." Position statement. Washington, DC: NAEYC. www.naeyc.org/resources/position-statements/dap.

NAEYC. n.d. "Principles of Effective Family Engagement." www.naeyc.org/resources/topics/family-engagement/principles.

Nguyen, U.S., S. Smith, & M.R. Granja. 2018. "Helping Early Care and Education Programs Assess Family Engagement Practices and Plan Improvements: Results of the Georgia Family Engagement Planning Tool Pilot". New York: National Center for Children in Poverty, Mailman School of Public Health, Columbia University. http://nccp.org/publications/pdf/text_1215.pdf.

Nitecki, E. 2015. "Integrated School–Family Partnerships in Preschool: Building Quality Involvement Through Multidimensional Relationships." *School Community Journal* 25 (2): 195–219.

NYSED (New York State Education Department). 2019. "The New York State Prekindergarten Learning Standards: A Resource for School Success." Albany, NY: NYSED. www.p12.nysed.gov/earlylearning/documents/new-york-state-prekindergarten-learning-standards.pdf.

OPRE (Office of Planning, Research, and Evaluation, Administration for Children and Families). 2011. "Family–Provider Relationships: A Multidisciplinary Review of High Quality Practices and Associations with Family, Child, and Provider Outcomes." Issue Brief OPRE 2011-26a. Washington, DC: OPRE. www.acf.hhs.gov/sites/default/files/opre/family_provider_multi.pdf.

Owen, M.T., J.F. Klausli, A. Mata-Otero, & M.O.B. Caughy. 2008. "Relationship-Focused Child Care Practices: Quality of Care and Child Outcomes for Children in Poverty." *Early Education and Development* 19 (2): 302–329.

Pan, T. 2018. "Study on the Influence of Exercise on Children's Cognitive Learning Ability." *Educational Sciences: Theory and Practice* 18 (5): 1940–1947.

Pate, R.R., & J.R. O'Neill. 2012. "Physical Activity Guidelines for Young Children: An Emerging Consensus." *Archives of Pediatrics and Adolescent Medicine* 166 (12): 1095–1096.

Powell, D.R., S.-H. Son, N. File, & R.R. San Juan. 2010. "Parent–School Relationships and Children's Academic and Social Outcomes in Public School Pre-Kindergarten." *Journal of School Psychology* 48 (4): 269–292.

Pratt, M.E., S.T. Lipscomb, & S.A. Schmitt. 2015. "The Effect of Head Start on Parenting Outcomes for Children Living in Non-Parental Care." *Journal of Child and Family Studies* 24 (10): 2944–2956.

Ruprecht, K., J. Elicker, & J.Y. Choi. 2016. "Continuity of Care, Caregiver–Child Interactions, and Toddler Social Competence and Problem Behaviors." *Early Education and Development* 27 (2): 221–239.

Schmit, S., & H. Matthews. 2013. "Better for Babies: A Study of State Infant and Toddler Child Care Policies." Washington, DC: Center for Law and Social Policy. www.clasp.org/resources-and-publications/publication-1/BetterforBabies2.pdf.

Sosinsky, L., K. Ruprecht, D. Horm, K. Kriener-Althen, C. Vogel, & T. Halle. 2016. "Including Relationship-Based Care Practices in Infant-Toddler Care: Implications for Practice and Policy." OPRE Report # 2016-46. www.acf.hhs.gov/sites/default/files/opre/nitr_inquire_may_2016_070616_b508compliant.pdf

Suizzo, M.-A., L.E. Tedford, & M. McManus. 2019. "Parental Socialization Beliefs and Long-Term Goals for Young Children Among Three Generations of Mexican American Mothers." *Journal of Child and Family Studies* 28 (10): 2813–2825.

Velez-Ibanez, C.G. 1988. "Networks of Exchange Among Mexicans in the U.S. and Mexico: Local Level Mediating Responses to National and International Transformations." *Urban Anthropology* 17 (1): 27–51.

Virmani, E.A., A.-M. Wiese, & P.L. Mangione. 2016. "Pathways to Relational Family Engagement with Culturally and Linguistically Diverse Families: Can Reflective Practice Guide Us?" In *Family Involvement in Early Education and Child Care*, ed. J.A. Sutterby, 91–115. Vol. 20 of *Advances in Early Education and Day Care*. Bingley, UK: Emerald Publishing Limited.

Wolf, E. 1966. *Peasants*. Englewood Cliffs, NJ: Prentice-Hall.

Wright, T.S. 2011. "Countering the Politics of Class, Race, Gender, and Geography in Early Childhood Education." *Educational Policy* 25 (1): 240–261.

Yahya, R., & E.A. Wood. 2017. "Play as Third Space Between Home and School: Bridging Cultural Discourses." *Journal of Early Childhood Research* 15 (3): 305–322.

Yang, W., & H. Li. 2019. "Changing Culture, Changing Curriculum: A Case Study of Early Childhood Curriculum Innovations in Two Chinese Kindergartens." *Curriculum Journal* 30 (3): 279–297.

Zauche, L.H., T. Thul, A.E.D. Mahoney, & J.L. Stapel-Wax. 2016. "Influence of Language Nutrition on Children's Language and Cognitive Development: An Integrated Review." *Early Childhood Research Quarterly* 36 (3): 318–333.

About the Author

Marie Masterson, PhD, is the Director of Quality Assessment at the McCormick Center for Early Childhood Leadership at National Louis University. She is a licensed early childhood teacher, a national speaker, child behavior expert, and author of multiple books and articles that address behavior guidance, parenting, early care and education, and high-quality teaching. She was previously a university professor in early childhood teacher education and early childhood specialist for the Virginia Department of Education.

Index

Page numbers followed by an f refer to figures; those followed by a t refer to tables.